ANALECTS

ANALECTS

MICHAEL GESSNER

BLAZEVOX[BOOKS]
Buffalo, New York

ANALECTS
by Michael Gessner
Copyright © 2019
Published by BlazeVOX [books]

Interior design, Cover design and typesetting by Geoffrey Gatza
Cover Image: image courtesy of the Metropolitan Museum of Art
  Faience Wedjat-eye amulet
  Period:Third Intermediate Period
  Date:ca. 1090–900 B.C.
  Credit Line:The Cesnola Collection, Purchased by subscription, 1874–76
  Accession Number:74.51.4526

First Edition
ISBN: 978-1-60964-348-5
Library of Congress Control Number: 2019939459

BlazeVOX [books]
131 Euclid Ave
Kenmore, NY 14217
Editor@blazevox.org

publisher of weird little books

BlazeVOX [books]

blazevox.org

21 20 19 18 17 16 15 14 13 12 01 02 03 04 05 06 07 08 09 10

BlazeVOX

Acknowledgements

Grateful acknowledgment is made to those publications in which the following first appeared, or from which excerpts have been selected.

American Letters & Commentary: "American Migrations"
Asphodel: "Tree Garden"
BlazeVOX: *The Writers' Circle*
Echo Arcade: *Glass*, and from *On Location, Essays of Place*, "Battle of Picacho Peak," "Genii Loci," "Landings"
The Ekphrastic Review: "Sanitarium on the Wissahickon," (an excerpt from the same title that appeared originally in *The Edgar Allan Poe Review*)
FutureCycle Press: *Selected Poems*, "The Poem of Death," reprinted in digital archive by The Poetry Foundation, and "Braidings"
Gray's Sporting Journal: "Hunting the Thumb"
Jacket2: "Transitionary framings, a case"
Kenyon Review: "The Synecological Poem"
New Oxford Review: "Praying for a Nun"
North American Review: "To History—," "Authorial Intentionality and the Blue Delphinium"
The Satirist: "The Canadian Solution"
Windover "Genii Loci"

CONTENTS

ANALECTS

*. . . the endless study of an existence, which is
the heroic subject of all study.*

—Wallace Stevens

MONOLOGUES

&

CUPULES

How is it that mind is capable of imagining mind? How can it describe its passions as if they were the same as external actions themselves? Or to assess, judge, accept or decline those behaviors that issue from it, knowing all the time it is imagining another self that understands all thought leads to its own, ongoing quest?

We talk to ourselves. Apart from referential collaborations, if the world listens at all, it is only a transitory hearing. Even in the Great Conversation, discourse on interiority is rarely met with regard; it is often discarded, or viewed as an unwanted distraction to the advances of science, mathematics, technology, cosmology, and new forms in every discipline. What remains, the classics, the cultural cannons, innovation in art, are noted by a scarce few, and usually for the scant span of an adult life, and if passed on through generations, each passing year brings them closer to replacement and in turn given over to the hands of time where they eventually become invisible. Should they survive, as in the case of Plato, Mencius, Christ, Boethius, Montaigne or Vyasa, they come down to us so modified by the absorption of marginalia, the well-intended but often inadequate paraphrase unique to translation, or with commentary that is only commonplace and reveals nothing but the astonishment of the uninformed reader who added it in the first place, and other interpretations over successive generations, that we cannot determine with any accuracy their authorship and must accept the descriptions of thoughts and deeds as an amalgam of attributions. In the meantime, and in general, the world is much too busy with its own daily concerns to have the curiosity or luxury of spending time with the art of interiority of any kind. Historically, this has been the case. And over time we will become what our ancestors left, cupules; collections of enigmatic cyphers unique to what once was.

Two hours' drive northwest from our home in Tucson, Arizona there are about 40 rock outcroppings with a variety of petroglyphs etched into basalt boulders by the ancients who once inhabited the region, the Hohokam and the Patayan. Some date from 7,500 BCE and some have cupules.

Cupules are considered the oldest form of rock art, and required a good deal of energy and time to create. Although associated with funerary and fertility rites, they have also been regarded as patterns of serious intent that cannot be understood or appreciated without knowing the ethnographic beliefs of their creators. These cup-like impressions represent the earliest known art forms and date from 700, 000 BCE.

At the Arizona site, near Gila Bend, cupules of a more recent origin are mixed with images of hunters, rabbits, foxes, birds, circle-mazes, dwelling grids, various life, death and resurrection glyphs. All of these, taken together, may be considered only as artifacts of human experiences deemed important enough to have created them in the first place. In any case, they come to us as fragments of a past we cannot fully appreciate or experience in absence of their larger historical and cultural contexts.

When I had written an early mentor, the American poet, W. D. Snodgrass in the late 1990s recalling the perfections of his poem, "Monet: 'Les Nymphéas,'" which I had taught in honors colloquium classes for years without his knowledge, he responded: "How very kind of you to write me about my Monet poem . . . . I must say that receiving such a letter is the one thing that can make the hard work of writing worthwhile; if I owned a stone wall I would carve your letter there." The impulse, perhaps necessity, to carve ourselves into rock—even as a metaphor of permanence; painted hands on cave walls, Sumerian cuneiforms, Egyptian hieroglyphs, the monoliths of Ahimsa, the Thunder Stone and the Western Stone, Trajan's column, the great obelisks and cenotaphs, engraved temples of Poseidon, Apollo, Hadrian's wall, Yeats' tower, the mountain retreats of Hesse and Rilke, Jeffers' Tor House—persists in us.

We use stone to memorialize our passions and ourselves. Our cities stand as necropolises with statues human and divine, fountains, obelisks, friezes, and far too many buildings embellished with famous busts, images of statesmen, and explorers. Cemeteries are cities of headstones. Stone sculptures of one form or another have never gone out of fashion, and have survived the birth and extinctions of a great many languages.

Still our passions search for a home more durable than the body from which they've sprung. That too, has not gone out of fashion. It's deep in the yearning of our species. Here it has taken the form of print and paper. Our most integrated arts, like poetry, ostensibly a synthesis of all the arts, seem to be the most vulnerable to the damaging effects of time. In the case of language, electronic media storage and retrieval systems are not enough; there must be (ongoing) successful diachronic translation, and along with other visual or aural knowledge, must rely on the stability of electro-magnetic fields. We struggle so much to survive. Or perhaps, we struggle so much for our artifacts to survive, thinking they will somehow echo ourselves in our absence.

We are, each of us, a monologue. It may be said with confidence that our species is itself a monologue; that is, although its members converse among themselves, share knowledge, decline or progress as a result, the sum of our speech is alien to the universe. We may claim we are speaking for it, or some of our more elegant mathematical equations appear to disclose or predict geological and celestial events, but our communication—all of it—is an idiom in a box set aside from whatever relationships the earth and the cosmos have through means (physical, chemical,) that we can only observe, record and speculate upon—human utterings with which the cosmos doesn't seem to concern itself. So whatever we may make of ourselves, or the world, is made for the benefit of our human brothers and sisters, and no other. The correspondence among living things does not include our languaging. We may say 'the world is absurd,' but this is just another way of saying, absurdity is a concept unique to us, to our species and otherwise is without meaning. It is a comment on the limits of our knowledge and our understanding. And yet, as soon as we seem to connect with a thing, we depart only to attach ourselves to another, only to depart again, and so on, like a perpetual chain of perceptual events.

We are compelled to leave something of ourselves, no matter how rare or perishable. The yearning for permanence is perhaps the single most salient aspect of our species, and should our creativity contend for that position, we might say much of creativity itself seems concerned with the quest for permanence, perhaps through proliferation and variation. But permanence of what, exactly? Movement? Ourselves? The natural world? Or something else we can't quite explain?

In any case, comic or serious, crude or refined, these commentaries have been of sufficient personal appeal to warrant inclusion here. Many offer notes on writing and the writer; poets and poetry. Collectively, these might serve as a reference guide for those who wish to travel the writer's psyche, although it may never be known if they hold the same significance for others; that they may never create paratexts or metatexts, they have fulfilled their function, which was the expression of the form and energy that created them in the first place, that urged them into existence, even if in the end they take their place among the myriads of lost notebooks, so very much like the cupules themselves; mute monologues.

Tucson, Arizona
June, 2019

JOURNAL EXCERPTS

—When entering the dance hall of Poetry, what the poet must learn
to accept, and cannot accept, is that Poetry is always looking for
another dance partner.

—If a poet expects more from a poem than it gives by its occasion,
by its own graces, then the poet expects too much. The poet's prize
is the poem. The poet should understand this from the beginning.
Positions, awards, public honors, will steal honest purpose and joy
from the poem itself, which should remain the center of all other
things that are only its satellites.

—Why must life become a moral essay?

— The poet is taken from the determined biological path (birth,
procreation, death, the quotidian realities,) on the Grand Detour.
The life of a poet may be seen as one of detours. The exploration
and the connection of them is a life's work. ("Authorial
Intentionality and the Blue Delphinium")

—If it does not curl itself naturally into blanket or leaf, then let it
stand naked, alone, let it speak directly.

—The suffering that has occurred from confusing sin and biology is
immeasurable.

—Tragedy is vanity.

—We should never feel sorry for a writer. If he is bad, he doesn't deserve it. If he is mediocre, it doesn't matter. If he is good, then he has touched the face of God and doesn't need it. This thought alone should console him and if it doesn't, he suffers from a character flaw so deep it cannot be healed, and for this should never be pitied.

—All too frequently, the application of grammar puts braces on the runner.

—Creations are born from vigor and flawless vision, a discovery of some perfection in absence of any anxiety, judgement, or analysis.

—The shape of the sublime is found in the spiral. Its sensation is silk sliding over the forearm.

—I have gone to meet absence.

—Does the Arboretum need another weeping willow?

—What expectations should we have of a life condemned from its beginning?

—I am always surprised when those things that disgust me are treasured by others.

—Poetry is the fortune that often lies in a closed account, the one with our name on it, the one we cannot spend in the material world.

—In his conclusion to "Multiplicity," (*Six Memos for the Next Millennium*,) Italo Calvino spoke of what was closest to his heart:

> Think what it would be to have a work conceived from
> outside the self, a work that would let us escape the limited
> perspective of the individual ego, not only to enter into selves
> like our own but to give speech to that which has no

language.

This could be considered a description of what is truly original, in the Ovidian sense, as both example and point of comparison. To speak of anything as original requires qualification and caution, but when invention exceeds the boundaries of the known then such qualifications are unnecessary.

—Poe is the Icarus of American Literature.

—Occasions create voice. They should; currents in water, air, human affairs, seasons and stars all are in perpetual change. If a voice is static, an overlay to every wild condition, then it is broken. The poet readily becomes a case of *Deja dit*.

—"Perhaps he is a fool, in the way an ethical man is a fool, and if he is a fool, he is a noble fool," Reynold to Chester Dorn, of Desmond O'Dell, a 19th century labor leader (characters from a work in progress.)

—When Dickinson writes "Wild Nights, Wild Nights" she does not only speak for the cosmos, she *is* the cosmos.

—Much too often, just about everything related to my body is a nuisance.

—One of the jobs of older people is to tell the young how much they admire them, even when they are foolish.

—We are all orphans. Human communities, at heart, are orphanages.

—Anyone can enjoy an expensive thing. But to enjoy a cheap thing that is only mediocre requires a rich imagination. Corollary#1: Anyone can smoke a cheap cigar, but it takes someone special to actually enjoy a cheap cigar. Corollary # 2: If you can find something cheap, and it is better than it would be otherwise because of its cheapness, then you have found something better than the best.

—Ideally, writers are best when read, not seen.

—Fables, narratives, lives, begin with grievance. Events—cosmic and human—are created by, and in discontent.

—Rilke, when writing Kappus, addresses the seriousness of the world, ". . . and everything is serious," when Hesse, his contemporary, returns again and again to the celestial laughter of Mozart and Goethe.

—If popular culture continues in its current trends, and there is not much to indicate otherwise, and with the celerity of the growing sense of the transtemporal in an increasing profusion of electronic images and electronic communications, we will think of ourselves as fictions; there is no actual self, only an illusion-of-self. A replacement reality. It will make no difference if we live fifteen seconds, or 150 years. Before the electronic age, the memory of a narrative event, fictional or real, was significant and could last a lifetime. This is no longer the case; narratives have shorter and shorter life spans, crowded out by other narratives, a cluster of blips on a screen blinking on and off, whether they are 'real' life experiences, imagined, or some combination. This phenomenon becomes greater as the population of our species continues to increase and our relationships, actual and electronic, become more and more transitory. Even now we are seeing this trend escalate into the fragmentary, the impulsive, and the immediately forgettable. The volume of memory storage and retrieval of electronic data may offer an antithesis, or antidote for some; however it remains to be determined whether sheer volume will so decrease individuality as to make it insignificant.

—How much should we reproach ourselves, given that we are in large part the result of someone else's imagination?

—Subject subsumes object. No art is objectless, any more than it is subjectless. Subject is determined by choice, and even if made unconsciously, it is not without intent, as intent is not always a conscious act, just as choice may not be a conscious act. Choice is required in all art, and the product of choice is subject.

—An experimental writer writes for an imaginary audience, (which may include no audience at all.) When that writer has found similar writers, it is a great discovery.

—How human culture comes around to celebrating what it once disowned; disowning what it once celebrated.

—Species is theme. All else is variation, and this is how variation becomes everything.

—The Modern History of Publishing should be read synonymously with The History of Exploitation. With the exception of a handful of independent publishers, never has the use of capital been more abused than in the commercial publishing industry. Electronic print and the electronic press mark have liberated writers of the 21st century.

—Generally speaking, contemporary popular poetry is the poetry of the cul-de-sac. When it moves at all, it moves in circles. It is not evolutionary. If it appears unique, is does so only because its readers do not recognize its similarity (in form, content, or sensibility,) to other (contemporary and earlier) popular poetries.

—So much of the Beat movement, (here I'm thinking of Corso's comments on the status of the [beat] poet as king or emperor,) is the attempt to create a carnival of symphony hall. We might imagine this would be a failure, even a laughable one, and aesthetically that may be the case, but in terms of popular reception, it has proven to be the opposite.

—Other than the grand passions that dispossess the mind of anything but themselves, or those incalculable and unavoidable vicissitudes, I should like to think of my existence as a mote floating in the aura of a cosmic Presence, the eternal redivivus of the cosmic Christ, both companion and essence of the ideal, of eternal goodness and beauty.

—What is there that wants us to be known? What desires our presence beyond ourselves without which there would not be . . . desire itself, the globe mallow and lupine . . . ("The Battle of Picacho Peak")

 —There is something to be said for getting through life as quietly as possible.

—When faced with originality in any art form, first responses are often bewilderment and discomfort. We may sense this, and we know our best literature is never far from the spoof, the hoax, the put-on, and this is the risk—and the gamble—[for both reader and author.] ("The Synecological Poem")

—The things I haven't done, and at times, wish I had, are those things, had I done them, would be to my lasting regret. This regret—from the doing—would be much worse than any regret from not doing.

—Generally speaking, when a reader cannot discuss adequately the meaning of a text because of time, or effort required, or as is most often the case, simply because he is challenged by the concepts he may find there, he talks about faults in grammar. This is like evaluating *haute cuisine* by discussing tableware.

—The functional (or operational) imagination is an extension of the primal imagination—neither Coleridgean or Jungian—which drives every quest and questor, and should it include Kant's intuition, and then it is an anticipatory intuition of the grandiose, a central image collaborating as the emergent companion with the images we experience of the world, in its every cell, every shape of rock, every word, every movement made. Imagination's image is agent and agency.

—Among literate generations, those who have sought learning and entertainment from written texts, the love of the book, the printed paper in the hand, the sense of the spine, for them these things in sum may have become epigenetic in their attraction. What else would adequately explain the insistence on their perpetuation?

—For a work of literature to become truly successful, the reader must become it. The body must absorb its essence.

—Death was in the mind/ before thought or love, / in ourselves and in our lovers. ("The Poem of Death")

—The transgender/queer poets seek to change language as a communally-shared reference as they have sought to change themselves, insofar that is possible, that is, their own gender identity, thus he, she, and/or it, become(s) 'they,' which forces language itself to embrace multeity. Personal and linguistic alterity may be the most attended subjects of our period, alongside those of ecology.

—The pursuit of any art form carries with it the likely probability, perhaps an assurance that the artistically inept will find their way if only among their brothers as there are so many of them; the mediocre will be praised; the talented adored, and the gifted, as often as not, will be ignored, by-passed by the others in the art race. Art—however it is presented in its *milieu*, and in its time—is less about art and more about the artist, school, life narrative including current, past or possible future relationships, obligations, exchanges, ethnic, gender, and social politics. The Art Thing itself is seen through these images. After a time has passed, and all the frenzy ceases, the Art Thing should be itself. Ideally it should be this; standing alone in the museum or on the page without critics, or accolades. Art should be evaluated only after everyone associated with its creation has been dead for several generations. And it should not be re-introduced to new generations by cultural movements or organizations created for the sole purpose of perpetuation. So it has been that whenever we are first introduced to the work of an artistic figure, that figure stands behind the work, but more often, next to it, and with some (curious) regularity in front of it. The figure often has a personal narrative that as human drama catches and holds our first attentions. To everyone's misfortune, art often first becomes known, and is frequently sustained through non-art relationships, narratives, social and cultural exchanges of the artist during his lifetime.

—There is, in our finest moments the sense of elevated peace, a divine harmony which all life and nature have coordinated in some way to produce. (I think of Willa Cather's narrator in *My Antonia* in the garden becoming "something entire.") This experience may be without anything other than its own (unaccountable) associations, or accepted as a consequence of cataclysms. If we deny this phenomenon, or assume this condition as a nominal occurrence only; not worth the great disasters which have either produced it or are woven around it, or accompany it with active involvement, or in their temporary absence, then it lessens our condition considerably.

—Most people most of the time are quite ready to say anything about anything—or anyone.

—The holiest among us are those who see holiness in others. The most beautiful are those who see beauty in others. Thus the faithful who worship saints—living and dead—are themselves saints unknown to themselves.

—Wallace Stevens, in a letter dated March 21, 1907 wrote to Elsie Moll: "To be young is all there is in the world. The rest is nonsense—and cant." This is as impressive as W. H. Auden's line from "In Memory of W. B. Yeats," that "Poetry makes nothing happen," and both are not only powerful declarations—flashes of heat lightning— but also astonishing half-truths, at best, and at worst, two of the most unfortunately memorable and misleading lines from two significant 20th century poets. Auden does seem to mitigate his statement later in his poem, however for Stevens, there is no such augmentation.

The young are for the most part unaware of the glories of youth; they only come around to recreating them some years later, as in the case of the 27 year-old Stevens. What irony there is in the reflection of what the imagination has built; a palace from a common house. Thus, these all-inclusive views, to be anything at all, rely on reflection's reconstruction. In Stevens' declaration, we might embrace his sentiment, for we do remember such a time, in most of our lives, when youth was everything, but that was rarely in its living, and only in its recollection.

The romantic attraction is not as immediate, or is it as uncomplicated, as found in Auden's line, "Poetry makes nothing happen." The idea that poetry itself occurs, that it does happen, and that nothing happens cannot happen, may be brushed aside quickly as obvious contradictions that damage the message. What is a curiosity, if not a fascination, is Auden's return in prose and interview to this notion of poetry as an agent of material change, of alteration in human events, of being a cause of physical reaction. It's as if he wanted to think of the poem as a mechanical device that sets other events or objects in motion. That it would operate like a lever, or a tool. Had this been a one-time statement, it could be dismissed on the grounds of a bad day; disgust with one's art, (natural enough from time to time, and forgivably human,) but it was otherwise; Auden returned to his declaration; it never seemed to leave him, or was it ever modified.

Among the many responses to this position, two beg attention: there are in reliable accounts of recorded history, incidents of poetry actually changing historical events.

In her memoir, Nadezhda Mandelstam recalls a statement made by her husband, Osip: "Only in Russia is poetry respected, it gets people killed. Is there anywhere else where poetry is so common a motive for murder?" Mandelstam's death—a result of poetry— should emphasize the point that poetry does make things—one might say everything—happen. Surely the number of poets we have not read, that will remain unknown, have, like Mandelstam, died for what they said, and what they said against various regimes or individual despots, has been—like the poets themselves—often obliterated from history.

Poetry has either introduced, or been associated with social justice issues relative to human rights, gender, race, labor conditions, and other inequalities, and has acted in such a way as to improve those conditions. The poetry of William Blake, Elizabeth

Browning, Edwin Markham, and Paul Laurence Dunbar, serve as ready examples and should underscore the point.

Lastly, that poetry makes something happen is not simply a material response; human actions that change the outward lives of others, but also the nonmaterial, as when one comes away from a poem altered, having experienced the transformations of the poem.

—Thirty or 40 years ago, most published verse at all notable, rewarded, or promoted, was well-worked academic verse indistinguishable from other academic verse and remains a monotone among monotones, which some poets still practice today. But much of that cultural drift has been redirected by a suspiciously similar volume of poetry that has innovation-for-its-own-sake as its guidon. As with its predecessor, one rarely finds a distinguished voice, profile, or passionate stance. Oddity alone then becomes the quest, and oddity may have merit when embracing transtemporal realities—*sub specie aeternitatis*—but rarely when examining our daily, passing attentions.

—Much poetry in our age in the English-speaking world is so pathologically self-absorbed with petty concerns; it may be collectively regarded as a poetic era of convolution; the poetry of specious attachments.

—Oddity is accepted not only as a condition of originality, but *as* originality. Peculiarity itself has become a valued trait pursued by those who would not be noticed without it. Such peculiarity may be the development of various syntheses in the arts, random designs, abnormal behaviors, or the result of birth or socio-economic class. The wealthy may be adored, or feared, envied or ignored, but they are rarely pitied. We have yet to acquire any true compassion for the

rich, of those born into excessive wealth. We do not understand
their poverty. They know this, and they know they have been
exiled from the human community of shared compassion, and they
know they will never be able to change this, and so they live in
isolation from the true, unconditional affections of others.

—Most human enterprises, including art, are produced by
misanthropes. Usually there is some chronic wrongness that irritates
or angers an individual. Of course, we come by this naturally
enough; nature has its needs. If we are not fed or we do not sleep,
we are disagreeable, so much so, that we might think all of our
existence is motivated by the discomforts of need. This biological
list of necessities extends to psychological desires—the need to
discover then discard companions, lovers, to leave one organization
to join another, the acquisition of newer appliances, homes, cars,
and so on—and thus we find such underlying discontent in our
literature. It too, extends itself into areas of the required Thing: the
offence of injustice, may apply to much of our art, certainly
literature, and poetry. However, there is, within the human being
the capacity to experience what might be called perfection. It is that
assurance, elevated and secure, of well-being with oneself and with
the world, even tho' the world is in turmoil. Perfection needs no
cause. It is sustained by its own presence. To live in this, as much
as one possibly can, seems to me to contain sensible purpose;
purpose in sense. It is what Auden found most desirable in the
poetry of Dylan Thomas. However, it should be noted that even the
most tragic poems are brightly shrouded in overly-worked, often
elegant diction.

—If we were to distill what is known by that memorable phrase 'the
human condition,' to its most salient feature, or to assign its most
deserving theme, it would be abandonment.

The human being, once capable of reflectivity, considers itself as having been abandoned from Paradise, the Womb, and into a world of continual need, fraught with terrors. Later, the individual perceives abandonment from parents as they depart, and perhaps other family members, and should that person live long enough, there is the abandonment of one's spouse. Behind all of this is this life's message: it will abandon us as individuals, and eventually our species itself to nothingness, to the night.

Abandonment—fear or apprehension of it— is at the center of every disaffection, and every doubt, or vulnerability. The awareness of abandonment places the human in a state of *horror vacui*. It is this state from which we flee at its every suggestion. That, or we become so weak from it, we surrender to it. It may manifest itself in war, other conflicts, or misogyny, which should not be seen as a justification in principle or practice, but only help to explain their reoccurrences in military and cultural history.

Various reaction formations emerge from abandonment and may create marvelous ensembles of consolation.

Disequilibrium is the anodyne to emptiness, and to that vacuity created by abandonment. Our worst and best fascinations are expressed from disequilibrium. Thus we wander from person to person, location to location, searching from one thing to another.

—On being asked by a local poet to attend with him an open microphone reading at a favorite restaurant and bar (Hotel Congress in Tucson). My reply:

I think you should go. My thinking has always been my thinking on this. Public readings are of three kinds: a) impulsive, that is, a lark—a gathering of a few (or more) poets at a bar one evening and one might recite from memory an amusing poem, or b) an open session, or c) an invited reading.

Unlike a) or b), an invited reading suggests there is some interest in the poet or the poet's work. Otherwise, it is a case of poets pushing themselves onto others in an open reading, others who really don't care, and are only present to hear themselves read, and receive (mechanical) applause from those who wish the same for themselves, and operate from that concern, which does no one any good, least of all the reader. It's a pretentious illusion.

Yes, and there's even a predictable list of poet-types who read at open-mic readings: the timid homebody who admits she's unsure of herself or her verses (supplication for sympathy and acceptance,) encouraged by one or two other timid homebodies who've come to cheer her on, the loudmouth crank who usually has a political axe to grind, the clown who's made up some rhyming witty thing, (hiding behind the lighthearted; the loss won't be as great) who thinks he is amusing, when others don't, and only emit a compulsory chuckle from the social pressure of the occasion, the neglected poet who was fair at his best and believes he has been unjustly persecuted by fate, etc., domestic philosophers who don't read a poem but deliver anything from a declarative aphorism to a diatribe of their own making in the most profound (theatrical) way, the obscurest poet who writes his great ideas in a linguistic closet that no one could possibly open, (the "Language" poets are wonderful examples) and the obligatory poet, someone of reputation (like a city poet laureate) who must be there, to do time, duty.

The whole affair is awkward, pretentious, and unnecessary.

Please don't ask again.

—If human suffering could be measured, it would weigh as much as the earth itself.

—Why do we pursue someone else's ambitions? Corollary: Although we may be the product of someone else's imagination, we should not be required to pursue someone else's agenda.

—Trees pre-existed our earliest forebearers by more than 350 million years, providing oxygen, food, shelter and protection to the present day. Their images are deep in the heart of our species, in its primal collective memory and resurface in its literature: the oldest Hellenic oracles listened to the rustlings of beeches and oaks to determine future actions; Daphne prayed to Gaia to be transfigured into what has become the noble and eponymous laurel, the fig tree under which Rome was founded, another that saved Odysseus from Charybdis' whirlpool; a third sacred fig, under which the Buddha attained enlightenment, the World Tree, or the Tree of Life, like the Yggdrasil, holding up the cosmos, connecting the heavens, the earth, and the underworld is found in the mythology of nearly every ancient human community. Each culture seems to have its sacred groves; characters of Shakespeare sought their consolation to expel sorrow, the transformative groves that populate Nigerian, Indian and Asian mythologies suggest a magical kinship, knowledge greater than sorrow, or what we know.

This mytheme, recurrent in so much of the romantic and nature poetry of the last several centuries, has increasingly populated the poetry of the past few decades as we have become painfully aware of the imminent dangers of deforestation, global warming, and the carbonization of the atmosphere, all of which have given rise to the subgenre of ecopoetry. ("The Synecological Poem")

—In the arts, the most enduring figures are large—by that I mean welcoming, generally caring, humane—and small figures are irretrievably (and painfully) small.

—If this were the only 'life' we would be so paralyzed by its finality, we could not do anything at all in its duration.

—A poem has its own body; it speaks.

—What is craft but a working-class term associated with labor, measurement, structure, and practical application? It was given great authority and widespread use in creative writing classes in America since the end of WWII when its universities were flooded with G.I. Bill students. Later, it gained popularity as creative writing programs developed to attract students of working-class families who wanted to become important writers, and who could sell the concept to parents worried about an uncertain future. Now, their sons and daughters were learning something, a craft. And this cannot be excused or elevated by associating the word with *poiema*, a thing made, or 'making,' and the poet becomes a material 'maker,' when the source is nonmaterial, the imaginative creation, *poiein*; creator. If by craft, creative writing teachers mean the concepts and uses of literary devices and forms then let them say so. However, these are artistic methods.

Collectively, as a concept, these do not constitute craft but rather artistic treatments. (Some might say subjects are capable of initiating or helping to form their own unique treatments, but this concept occurs only to rich imaginations.)

—Why are we driven to have our experiences outlast us? After all, they were never ours alone. Can they ever be repeated as they occurred? Perhaps there is some force beyond the awareness of mortality that drives us. Perhaps it is that notion of R. P. Blackmur; the frenetic compulsion to accumulate, to add the available stock of reality, as if Plenitude itself were some tireless ringmaster in an expanding universe.

—Who is to say that some of the wisest among us do not throw their lives away?

—If a writer has not become the thing he writes about, wait, he will. The writer lives in the world he creates. This is why the choice of Subject is critical. His own life lives in the life of his books. If the writer is a fantasist, anarchist, elitist, those will be primary in his writing; the interests of characters are his own. The subject is what is found most attractive in his own life, from which he cannot extricate himself. If a writer writes one book of fiction or poetry he has his autobiography. (Character is as much in voice as subject.)

The most demanding genres are perhaps ironically, the more strenuous: philosophy, biography (of deliberate lives—the philosopher-politician, devoted scientists, pioneers, explorers, and so on,) translation, (I cannot say enough about the translator's commitment, labor, and personal sacrifice,) and the writing of the literature of history, art, and possibly the most arduous and demanding; dictionaries, encyclopedias, and the great taxonomical systems found in natural sciences and linguistics, and writers of invention, those who catalogue their discoveries, (Freud, Galileo, Da Vinci, Montaigne, Proust, Benjamin are but a few examples.)

The dramas of loyalty, suffering through adversity, and justice require a different writer than the writer of entertainment for mass audiences—the writer of dungeons and dragons, gothic horror and fantasy, sado-masochistic pornography disguised in a quest of some kind or another. At the bottom of most of the writing to entertain, today at least, stands the figure of the Nadaist. This is no less true of much of the writing in the arts as well; that figure may be found in some of our most celebrated poetry and fiction. He has found nothing of value or meaning in his own life and his expressions are aligned with this complaint. Most "Language'" poets, Conceptualists, Flarfists, Deconstructionists, Dadaists, Absurdists,

Metalingual Satirists and Ironists are found in this category. They exist in the name, and never the purpose, of 'art'. They share similar marks: cynicism, a painful self-consciousness, the negation of every possible historical criterion of traditional or literary worth, and they delight in this as they delight in themselves.

Lastly, the writer, to be a writer must be able to accept failure, not only the failure of a work, or its design, or its intention, or its reception, but the failure of a life's work. The writer must transcend his own personal and emotional investments.

—We can create meaning only if we truly value the past; that we carry it with us in the shrine that is our mind. Attempts to dissolve the past surround us and are perpetuated by mind merchants, hoping to gain psychologically, politically, or financially from the evacuation of meaningful and personal experiences by replacing them with a ceaseless pattern of desire and acquisition for whatever they are promoting.

—Phonaesthetics: there is in cacophony elegance. The phonic lexicon. There is such a thing as sonic logic. In fact, sound itself may possess an animated logic in its modulations.

— A truly fulfilled life does not require itself to find any other expression of itself than itself.

—Our thinking, our concepts of ourselves and our place, have been determined by our perception of magnitude. Our species becomes, as a whole, less important as it grows in number and as its images of the universe tend to reduce its importance. As a species we have less importance—the sense of it ourselves—than our forebearers.

—Always there are others quite ready to tell us who we are.

—The Academy of American Poets is like Noah's Ark, attempting to save every possible articulation in every form, each and all of whom are equal in value and grace. Or like the United Nations, everyone is represented no matter how rich, poor or unable their state.

—Much literary translation, particularly in poetry, is improvisation. Of the 61 translations extant of Homer's *Odyssey*—12 in the first 18 years of this century alone—essentially all are creative responses to, or re-castings of, existing texts. These are largely sequential changes to diction and syntax, and not produced because of earlier inadequacies or imperfections, but rather from political and commercial motives. The explanation most often given to the public is to argue the necessity for contemporary cultural adaptation. In the case of translations of previously untranslated texts, the use of bi-lingual readers fluent in the source language is rarely noted.

In the translation of referential material, say in science or technology, translators are restricted from creative treatments, and are in most cases bi-lingual, arising from those necessities unique to transliteration.

—The best mornings are met with the distinct pleasant residue that follows sleep. And so are our best memories of our best days; distant trees deep in lazy autumn.

—We should not allow our image of the body to influence the thought it produces. Thought should live apart from its mortal life. If there is a purpose to the body other than life itself and its reproduction, it is to convey thought. What thought describes is alive when the body is not.

—The intention of the author who excludes the imagination of the reader excludes the reader.

—The primary effort of the ideal life should be to search for that presence that recurs, and that is the presence and source of all good; elegance, harmony, clarity, so that being may endeavor to live in that presence and coexist with the sublime in the hope of transcending the self. And when encountering the worst fears, desperations, failures, catastrophes, it is language that finds a way to counter pose, perhaps in some way, offers consolation beyond pain, suffering, and devastation. How St. John of the Cross wrapped himself in mystical language; an eternal home.

There's a growing number of those who cannot extricate themselves from a world view dominated by the destruction caused by natural catastrophes; Vesuvius, Karatoa, the five great extinctions, and now in the early stages of the sixth, tsunami obliterations of thousands in an afternoon, the great Asian famines, the African floods, pediatric oncology wards, child soldiers, slavery, and they know these oppose the concept of a loving, all-knowing, and all-powerful god. These realities cannot exclude the presence of an eternal companion. That companion shapes rational thought itself. Case in point: in a series of interviews with centenarians, an English woman, aged 103, living in a communal home by sea lost her twin daughters, and later a son, then her husband. She had no family, and yet was grateful for her memories of them. She reasoned that had they not been in her life, she would not have her sustaining and pleasurable recollections of them. Instead, there would only be emptiness. This appears to be romantic idealism, but nature itself, despite all earthly bouts of turmoil and devastation seems to have greater episodes of romantic love, spilling over itself with fecundity. When we are the consequences of romantic love ourselves, why would we repudiate it? Would that not be a theft of the self? And don't others fall in love with those who have fallen in love with the world?

—Celestial mechanics seem to be a case of bi-polar personality; lofty awe of all that is inspiring to despair of it all and destruction. It is cyclical, and during this cosmic epoch, expanding. The incidence of these extreme fluctuations occurs at an exponential rate. In this way the earth is a cell, a microcosm. Our planet mimics galaxies; the five great extinctions to date, and geomagnetic reversals are among the most notable examples, followed by periods of steady growth and calm, and even during these less volatile eras there are erratic eruptions, storms followed by relative silence. They should serve as instances of such a 'personality'.

—By now, you would think the human race would have tired of fighting with itself.

—If sensibility is unconscious, or say a form of the body's belief as experience is belief, a phenomenon of the present t(s)ense, then what do rationalists experience? If we look at rationalists on a spectrum, we may see at one (ultra-liberal) end the psychobiologist who considers only material origins of every phenomenon, and at the other extreme, the empirical researcher. In any case, the rationalist, so intent on material realities and their investigation, may exclude that sense that accompanies others. It is a sense that is complete in itself, a rounded wholeness, pleasing (as if its existence were the same and for the same;) it is the sense of Sense in Its service.

—One of the poorest arguments is the attempt of an old person to convince a younger one that he is not all that he appears to be.

—This year (2018) Valentine's Day and Ash Wednesday fall on the same day: we live only by consuming other living organisms; it cannot be otherwise. Ingested cells nourish others; communicate biochemically; a varied continuance. Whatever our reason makes of us, our purpose or our identity, it is faulty; what we often think true is untrue; that what we think of ourselves and the universe is, after all, only what *we* think. For all we know, the basis of our greatest inventions, the mechanisms by which we imagine alternative realities—reaction formations themselves—are from the built-in biological necessity to survive. If there is a study of greater importance than the study of the self-in-the-world it is the study of the life force, for it now only allows, but drives our fascinations and our pursuits in every mode of exploration.

—More often than not, life receives more than it deserves; takes more than it gives. I live with the fear that I will either do more and thus pitch myself onto the ledge of dissolution, or that I will not do enough and pitch myself onto the same ledge. The horror and shame of not having done enough; the folly and shame of having done too much is an ongoing debate.

—Since the Renaissance, every century has had an increasing number of reductionists in proportion to the general population. In our age, reductionism has seeped into the popular and cultural mind so much so that empathy itself is regarded with contempt; compassion inauthentic and laughable; transcendence seems to have been replaced with indeterminism and irony, and with the awareness of the escalating mass of human population and the speed of the electronic transmission of events, the image of the individual has all but been abandoned.

—Glowing. Luminous, the eyes of poets.

—Many literary journals have gone to publishing electronically; some continue in print with an online issue as well. Among them, there is the notion that the print edition is somehow "First Tier," whereas the online publication comes in second. I should think these might be reversed. After all, who is to say the book on the shelf is not as durable—or perishable—as electronic media?

This is similar in sentiment to the publish-on-demand method of printing copies of texts distinct from the traditional publisher who publishes and edition with a fixed number of copies. The POD publisher invests less and his return is greater for he does not require warehousing, controlled temperature, and the like. I suggested this to a publisher and was met with disdain; he continued to warehouse his editions in the desert paying more than he made from book sales in inventory, leasing the warehouse, and so on. In fact, I had purchased at our local (University of Arizona) book fair, a biography, took it home, and when I first opened it, the spine cracked because the glue had dried out in a warehouse that did not have temperature control. Later, I mentioned the POD alternative to him, and again, disdain. But his next title was published using the POD process. Likewise, the board of the Poe Studies Association chose to publish the latest edition of Poe's complete letters with a little-known Luddite press in New York. Result? Over $100.00 a copy, and at the time, an amount few Poe scholars could afford, and others, unwilling to pay. When I mentioned this to the PSA president suggesting using a press mark and a POD platform, I was met with a mixture of apprehension and disgust. In any case, digital publication should exceed print medium in its available duration, variety and number.

—John Updike, whose novels are portraits of middle-class life among the middle class in mid-century America, has attempted to defend his narrow and unimaginative treatment by noting a simple distinction between "reality" and "escapism," that is, if other novelists aren't writing about what is perceived as the minimally mobile, otherwise static lives of 'characters' struggling with boredom, those writers are somehow less than authentic, and escapist in nature. Boredom is Updike's great trope, his *raison d'être*.

There should be a scale for period writing, from what is most telling and worthy of reflection of a particular time, to what does not contribute to historical understanding, or cultural growth.

—The material world is a manifestation of a set of interrelated ongoing nonmaterial constants. What expresses energy? If it has no thing other than itself, then what determines the forms it assumes?

—The greater one's abilities; the greater one's humility. This is one equation of character.

— Color is to visual artists what words are to the poet: color is being. It breathes. What is true of color is also true of words.

—Forms in poetry originated as reflections of the shapes of ideation, and its rhythms, reflections of sensations.

—*Ombra mai fu* is perhaps the most durable short lyrical poem in all of literature; the apogee of the aboreal paean, if only for Handel's treatment of Minato's lines.

—Is oblivion not salvation? Is death not oblivion?

—Intelligence never prevented anyone from being a fool. This in itself should tell us something about intelligence: the individual who lives a temperate, productive, and deliberate life, albeit an anonymous one may possess a practical intelligence, which, after all, may be the most satisfactory, sensible, and rewarding of any.

—The more certainty one has on any subject, the more suspicious I become.

—Of extremes: we are as likely to die of anonymity as we are of identity. Likewise, we may die from lack of food, or die from overfeeding.

—Authentic compassion for others requires the precondition of grief of the individual.

—This is the only world that grieves. It may be the only world that is conscious.

—I have always been in love with this earthly paradise, and that is nothing new, but I've been in love with this *place*, not with what actually takes place here.

—Imagined reality is the first motive and sustaining principle of life; it is why the species continues. It is the basis of all quests, failures, disappointments, and victories.

—Death—the image of the corpse—is a hard argument.

—Body, you have created the literature of estrangement, damnation, and lament.

—Among my worst fears and fascinations is that the idea and act of justice is confined to the human species. That is, it does not exist elsewhere.

—Three great themes: love, destruction, labor.

—The effusiveness of groves, gardens, even human populations, suggests the world is quite willing to love itself to death.

—If allowed to continue, human evolution will offer the certainty of increasing awareness, novel applications of new disclosures and syntheses.

—Poetry is its own life form.

—Every surface reflects another. Every thing has a surface, even the reflection of a surface.

—The central meaning of our existence is the making of meaning.

—The Irish can ridicule the thing they love and love the thing they ridicule. Who but the Irish would agree that ridicule is a redemptive trope?

—Youth may not need or value ideas, but old men should never run out of them.

—With freedom there is little serious philosophy or poetry; without it, there is much, and this applies to states as to individuals.

—A timid man who is also a bitter man is the worst kind of man.

—In the arts, more are cursed with anxiety than blessed with talent.

—If our realities are fictions, then this notion of reality itself suggests it is a fiction.

—In this life, the chief instinct and obligation of the individual is to avoid terror.

—In the worst of times, we must remember that we have been loved. But it is also in the worst of times that we find ourselves emptied of it.

—The value of juvenilia is that it, like no other mode, offers nuances of a world from which it has just recently arrived, often recollected in drifty passages, haunting sensations that are with us only in youth then gradually fade with age to the furthest depths of our ability to recollect them.

—Ideally, poetry is a synthesis of all the arts, but never in proportion each to the other. One usually glides above, as others trail, and at times weave themselves, perhaps for a line or two, dethrone the leading trope, and on it goes; currents plaiting. ("Braidings")

—With the possible exception of a few historically isolated spiritual communities, any human organization—cultural, social, ethnic, economic, political or religious—will in relation to its unrest, subjugate, manipulate or exterminate any other group for any reason. And histories' reasons have been notoriously irrational and based in primal emotion. The power of a group rises in proportion to the diminution of other groups; in fact, it has been a historical condition of ascendance.

—There seem to be several rather general classes of thought: the commonplace, consisting of empty platitudes and other notions that find their way into speech, often repeated until they are not worth saying at all; the illogical and banal, so difficult to endure, and that which is unique, offering some insight to a condition or problem.

Likewise, there seem to be several rather general classes of human beings (to which the classes of thought might correspond): the consumer, the contributor, and the creator. Unlike the classes of thought which are more contained, these categories may overlap; a contributor, say a factory or postal worker, pharmacist, or technician, must consume, but not solely, whereas the consumer's main activity is in the process of acquiring basic needs. The creator consumes less than either in proportion, and produces unique discoveries, inventions, processes, that require contributors to perform or operate (as with systems.) The backbone of cityscapes, of architecture, government buildings, the boulevards of the metropolis, and so on, is the worker-contributor, which I suspect, occupies a greater portion of our population than his other brothers—the consumers or the creators. However, were it not for the creators, we would be living in a non-evolving world, circular in motion until its extinction.

—We are creatures of infinite belief. We are always in the service of the Possible. This applies to every thought, enterprise and event. There is always future's presence. If we focus on a project or a thought we soon turn to this: what will we do with it? What will become of it?

—The insistence of depending on the future has almost become complete. It has replaced the present. It is the new paradigm toward which we've been wending; no longer does history shape our future, (if it ever truly did beyond a few suggestions that were in most cases, ignored,) but rather shapes our present. It nearly occupies the entirety of our conscious mind.

—January, 2000, the first month of the new millennium and there is an eclipse and a wine-red moon. I wonder how much blood will be unnecessarily spilled in this century. Children's hospitals are routinely bombed by government air squadrons in the mid-east.

War Experience, a Case of Cultural Darwinism

—In 1964 at the age of 20, in my second year at Wayne State University, the Viet Nam War was underway and there was a massive recruitment effort and a national draft system. Although most students still had student deferments, I thought I could withdraw for a semester, return the following semester, and still avoid induction.

This didn't happen. A month after my withdrawal from university, I received my draft notice to report to Ft. Wayne, Detroit for my physical, and I knew I would be called up a few weeks later.

I attempted to volunteer for reserve status which meant four months of active duty—basic and advanced training—followed by six years of attending weekend drills and two-week summer camps. Of course, like most units, reserve divisions were subject to deployment. However, the reserve units were filled—all of them.

I reported to Ft. Wayne, took my physical and other tests with perhaps as many as 100 other men on a single morning, returned home expecting my notice to report for active duty to arrive any day.

Less than a week later, I received a call from Sgt. ______ (I've long since forgotten his name,) who asked if I would visit with Col.

Hagen, as he wished to see me. This was very strange, of course. My notion of the military was that I would not be *asked* to do anything, rather told, and why would a colonel wish to meet with me anyway? What was I but another recruit, one without any particular skill or ability that could be possibly used or valued by the military?

On arrival, I was escorted to an auditorium of some kind. I remember there were recruits coming and going through this area. I sat at a wooden desk across from Col. Hagen who explained to me—he had my file in front of him—that he had retired from active duty and worked part-time at the installation to help in the war effort and it was an opportunity made available to him, something in which he had interest. And so it went. He told me that I would be drafted. That was a certainty. In addition, I would be "cannon fodder," and I was surprised he used that phrase. It didn't strike me as something a loyalist might say. He wanted to know about my interests and my background.

Somewhere in the conversation I mentioned my wish to serve in the Army Reserves. "Reserves?" he said. "The reserves are filled. Besides, there's a backlog of 6,000 men on the waiting list."

Our conversation, for the most part seemed routine, and toward its conclusion, he tapped the file on his desk and said, "You did well on your exams," and gave a perfunctory smile.

I remember taking tests between the ENT exam, eye exam, stripping and walking around with clothes and shoes in hand, from one physical inspection station to another, and so on, but I really didn't recall much about it, other than pages of multiple-choice questions.

I thanked him for seeing me; we shook hands, and I left for home, thinking my active duty instructions would arrive shortly— where to report, the basic training camp to which I would be assigned, what to bring, and resigned myself to the reality as best I could.

Instead, about two weeks after my meeting with the colonel, I received a letter of assignment to the 70th Infantry Division Training, S-3, Intelligence, at Fraser, MI.

This was a reserve unit, but it was a 'special' unit, one that, while it could be called to combat duty, it would first report to one of the training facilities for one year, or a cycle, replacing the training staff that would be shipped overseas. Then, after a year, the same would happen to the training reserve unit to which I had been assigned, further distancing me from the war in Viet Nam.

Fortunately, during my service, from basic training and AIT at Fort Leonard Wood, MO, in the fall of 1964 to my honorable discharge in 1971, our unit was never mobilized.

Without military interest, without useable skills, or rank, I would have become an infantry soldier almost certainly subject to combat.

The rather casual conversation I had with a retired officer on a late spring afternoon changed the course of my life in ways I have yet to understand. I could have easily become a war casualty, and didn't. What of those 6,000 men ahead of me in the greater Detroit area, the ones that wanted reserve assignments, but never received them and were drafted into action? What of them? And why was I taken aside as it were, and assigned to a training division which was perhaps the safest of any service branch at the time with the exception of the National Health Service, or the Coast Guard?

Years later, when I was being given an eye exam by an ophthalmologist and learned he had been a Marine Major in Viet Nam, I told him about my experience. He said that all branches would regularly screen recruits and select those who might serve best in other capacities, then assign them based on their evaluations. I was surprised to hear this. My best man, Steven Chason, a Danforth scholar, had been drafted out of Kenyon College after all, and served as a foot soldier, a rifle infantryman in Viet Nam, sent out regularly on night patrols. It didn't square. Apparently, the government had periods when such screening was done, and periods when it wasn't.

Over the years I've come to think of this as a case of cultural Darwinism. I would say it was racist in nature were it not for so many other European-Americans who were drafted among those 6,000 men vainly waiting for a reserve assignment in Detroit, many of whom must have been African-Americans as well. So I was left with mixed emotions; I am grateful for being taken out of war experience for which I had no interest or passion, but I am haunted by my exception. Was it necessary? Was it just? Hardly. Did I— or did anyone—deserve it? But that question could just as well be asked of those drafted into an unwanted and unjust war. Somewhere—in some field, makeshift grave, vet's hospital, or VFW chapter—there is a man, one man, living or dead, disabled, or not, who replaced me.

—When I ask myself about music in the heart of poetry, I must look about and feel vibrations in plant life, drafts of wind, insects chirping, the tremolos of rustling woods or the cacophony of busy cities—every body in itself and in concert with other bodies—every organism including the human body—is an Odeon. Thus the poem must breathe; its breathing, a motion of music. A pulse, a body. Oh how we are forever—like the earth itself—making bodies.

—The best actors are not found in Hollywood; they are found in churches and law firms.

—It is more than curious that *Annus Mirabilis* and *Annus Miserabilis* sound suspiciously akin.

—In life as in art, one must be willing to give something of immense beauty and withstand having it ignored, disgraced, even destroyed, then be willing to give again yet another creation of beauty, and another. Something in this stays; strengthens over time.

—The epistemologist knows enough to ask the question, 'how is it, that of all possible relationships, it is this particular way?' Not why a thing exists as it does, but rather by what conditions; how is it this way instead of others, when those others are equally possible? This question should be asked of every observation and every explanation.

—The will—the life force—urges us to live longer, live at any cost. Reason asks 'why'?

— From the year of my birth until I was 17, I lived on Longfellow Avenue in a suburb of Detroit. As a child, each evening after my Mother tucked me securely in bed, she would read poems to me; she would read from Tennyson's Arthurian idylls which had been rewritten in a children's edition, a favorite for their lyrical exploits, or "Break, Break, Break," or "Crossing the Bar," which my Mother read sometimes in a whisper as if to herself. Then there were Fitzgerald's translations of the quatrains of Omar Khayyam, Longfellow's "Nature," or his "Cross of Snow," again in a whisper as if the words themselves were sacred, and selected stanzas from Whittier's "Snow-Bound," or the poem she had memorized and that won for her a ribbon in eighth grade when she was invited to recite it going from room to room for the benefit of her schoolmates, Leigh Hunt's "Abou Ben Adham," and even today I think I may yet be pursuing some mention in that angel's book of gold. And so it was a beginning; an opening to a phosphorescent world.

—How is it that we see our bodies in landscapes? How is it that low twin hills and a fissure resemble the *mons pubis*? Or a mushroom resembles the phallus?

—Poetry transforms to being when we become conscious of the world.

—The populist imagines the uniqueness of the experimentalist; the experimentalist imagines the following of the populist.

—We are in a chain and do not know the links just as we are inhabitants of an estate we have no knowledge of ever having visited.

—If we have the choice to create beauty, should we?

—In Gide's brief biography of Wilde, the author records an anecdote given him in conversation following Wilde's imprisonment, (recounted in *De Profundis*,) of how Wilde came to understand meaning, perhaps purpose, through pity. Sorrow for another's state might be preferred as a contrast to pity. Pity for others is only a consolation for ourselves and means nothing to another unless 1) the other knows of our grief, and 2) that such grief is as real as their own is for their own misfortune, and shared by this knowledge. Otherwise, to pity another is to arouse resentment, even contempt, as when one insults another by saying "I will pray for you."

—Among the most inadequate, and perhaps saddest, literary commentaries is W. H. Auden's epilogue to the Ellmann edition of *Epistola: In Carcere et Vinculis,* Wilde's own title to his prison letter, a passionately moving manifesto on humanism, one that will surely find its way among the great apologias of recorded history. I would like to think there would be a golden period of human understanding and compassion when Wilde's letter will find its place in the company of the epistles of the church, and Wilde himself, sainted for his gift of understanding the human condition, and his unique abilities in communicating it to the rest of humanity, thus elevating the sensibilities of the species.

Auden, adorable for his vulnerability, his enthusiasms, and his monolithic literary achievements which so define his age, dismisses half of Wilde's masterpiece in his introductory sentence: "Wilde on Jesus or redemption through suffering is as childish and boring as Gide on the same subjects, but Wilde on Bosie . . ." and goes on to devote the remaining essay on the relationship between Oscar and the petulant boy. This, not spiritual transformation and what that transformation means to human experience, is the fascination that dominates Auden's mind. If he had used Wilde's affair as a platform for his revelations as Wilde had, or used his prison experience as such a platform, perhaps there could have been some redemption, but this was not Auden's choice. In fact, even a cursory reading of the letter shows Auden simplified, if not misread, when he began with his opening statement on that childish equation about suffering, and then abandoned it without further explanation. I do not know of any significant or notable writing that crudely paraphrases a concern that dominates an essay, then leaves it without supportive documentation, examples, and so on. So Wystan, let me say to you what I said in another letter to the dead: "We forgive our saints for what they do/ just as we forgive you for being you." ("Plath's Father")

—I am always in pursuit of the next great project. The best of these, I've learned is forever hiding its name.

—We will rarely find the most notable lives lived in palaces, just as we will not find humanists there, but among the lowly, those who have found spiritual brotherhood.

—In graduate school, having read Propp's *Morphology*, I was taken by the prospect that mind may be narrative in nature, and operates on functional imperatives, shaped by our earliest physical actions. Events—beginnings, middles, and ends—occur in syntactic time. We are still stuck—we may be forever stuck—in the tenses. This narrative structure served well for purposes of utility: the construction of dwellings, food gathering and hunting, but I've always been suspicious of its use when it turns up to explain higher order phenomena. In fact, I look for it, and when it shows up, I tend to turn away from the message itself thinking it came out of, and is chained to, an inflexible linguistic (and therefore cognitive) structure that is primitive in nature and may account for questions that do not yield—cannot yield—acceptable answers.

The most salient example of this may be found in the statements of Stephen Hawking, perhaps the most scientifically formidable figure of our day, if not the most celebrated one. His assertions about time, shared by many colleagues, is that time (he does not define time, at least in his paper, "The Beginning of Time," just as he does not define 'universe,') has a beginning. (This beginning curiously suggests another painfully limited notion, the uncaused cause—we must have an end to have a beginning—and perhaps as laughable for its celebration as a profound discovery, and unless we are considering something like Eliot's "Four Quartets," childish.)

Hawking has insisted on several occasions that the beginning of the universe occurred 15 billion years ago, or thereabouts. (I do not understand how it is we can talk about the universe as all that exists when we do not know all that exists.) Stars, plants, animals, species, have beginnings and ends. Two weeks before Hawking died he predicted the death of the universe as stars run out of energy. This does not seem congruent with the Laws of Thermodynamics, the Conservation of Energy—that energy cannot be created or destroyed—but let's move on: there may be something of redemption in Hawking's late views of parallel universes, or multiverse(s).

In 2011 he proclaimed "Philosophy is dead." Scientific facts may be disclosed to humans by humans without the need for human thought concerning the impact on humans with respect to their implications or interpretations. Observations of operations exclude any other application other than those applications to other operations. A closed loop.

It is interesting to note that the spokespersons for science, those who regularly visit talks shows, appear in the news, or over various media, figures like Hawking, Neil DeGrasse Tyson, Carl Sagan, and others cannot extol the advances of science without vilifying 'god,' (and this reference usually goes undefined,) philosophy or mythology, including religions. These attacks in themselves diminish the importance we might otherwise attach to such scientific advances, and although we might understand the frustrations of science popularizers with those who adhere to literal biblical texts in the light of new scientific discoveries that often refute them, it remains an irony that most of humanity will go on with its gods and myths and philosophies. If a thing is grand it is not made more so by berating perceived adversaries. Science has taken the pulpit and has sadly submitted itself to the "either-or" fallacy. Science becomes the religion it despises. The proponents who seek to replace all other belief systems with science should begin by giving a thoughtful reading of Chardin, Kuhn, Popper, Okasha, among others.

With these rather bold narrative structures in mind, I had been developing a narrative grammar in which a set number of descriptors performed a set number of functions. I often discussed this with my major advisor who happened to have been a child musical prodigy. Together we spent our weekends seeking relationships between the elements of narrative grammar and elements of scale. We may have been moving toward a translingual theory of narrative constituent 'notes' based on function, but I can't recall. We had great moments—and great fun—with our syntheses.

We found an unused classroom in a building which housed various florae from botanical researchers, and one weekend, perhaps late on a Saturday evening, we had a breakthrough. The blackboards that occupied two walls were filled with our notations. We were both exhausted and agreed to call it a night, but wished to preserve what had been placed on the boards. This was before cellular 'phones so we could not photograph our expressions, and my advisor was convinced no one would be using the room, and just for caution's sake wrote in large letters the word: SAVE on each of the blackboards. When we returned to the university the following Monday we both stole away from our academic responsibilities and went directly to the room to develop our ideas and when we arrived, the blackboards had been cleaned. Not a mark remained. We concluded that some conscientious custodian we never expected to visit an unused classroom, had, and cleaned the boards disregarding my advisor's note to "Save" the material. "But why would he have done this?" I asked. My advisor shrugged, "Maybe he couldn't read," then looked at me with a droll expression which somehow placed our ambitions in their rightful place.

Our most precious attractions often have other destinies.

—In speech as in writing, the most prolific are often the least profound.

—Apricot sun . . . . Melon moon

—Mary Burritt (Christiansen) who as a child sat on the knee of Ezra Pound when he visited her father at the University of Salamanca, and whom I'd met in Boulder, Colorado one afternoon on the Pearl Street Mall, has in my estimation developed a poetry that exceeds all others in its ethereal quality. From *The Solera Poems*, ". . . Evenings are beautiful colors,/ the erotic trees,/ the sources, the places/ of art, that are more important/ than dispersed landscapes." Or this from *Above Dolce*, "Poplars sleep among walls./ Alone with yellow linen shades,/ silences yield to tears . . . . Solaria lie along north shores/ where elms, shading the fields,/ are swept into exile." The images seem to drift off the page and we with them.

—If our earthly forms appear impermanent, how is it that we are capable of imagining permanence? Not the permanence of a particular form or event; what the mind does in memory, or by various repetitions or syntheses, but the notion of permanence itself (without object or image?) To suggest this phenomenon is a reaction to the absence of permanence, does not offer enough foundation to justify it. It lacks epistemology, (and not epistemological idealism.) It would be like saying with Richard Dawkins the noted atheist, that spiritual elevation is an "illusion," when we do not consider that even an "illusion" constitutes valid experience-as-experience. For all else, the 'White Man's Disease' is the pursuit of permanence.

—We may include Noah's family with his zoo.

—How can disability be anything other than a mottled gift if it rushes its victims towards overcompensation, and thus overachievement?

—Innocence is an eternal beauty. Tragedy makes it more so.

—Whatever attracts or repels, near or far, painful or dear, only does so by contrast.

—Imagination perforates material reality. It is what pores are to a sponge. Without them, a sponge cannot be a sponge, rather a dense mass of some kind. In other words, it cannot be spongy, no more than material reality can be reality.

—Because certainty is a necessary condition of survival, when it is questioned, or worse, doubted, it creates wide-scale social discord as in our own era of distrusting every fact and every source of information. This is evident in our news media coverage. Denial has never been so popular.

—Although suffering is unavoidable, it is made worse if it is unnecessary. The most inhumane suffering is caused when one individual suffers, and because of this suffering, a second individual is afflicted, as in the case of a spouse's actions or condition, or the suffering of family members, as when a loved one acquires a terminal illness, birth maladies or the like, and others are forced live a wretched and unnecessary existence.

—To better know what we do not know, or to better sense it, we say what it is not.

—Those whom we wish most to impress are those who have most impressed us.

—The writer must be his own hero; the chances of being someone else's are remote.

—A compelling story is built and sustained by irrational acts. This may be said of life narratives. It may even be said of history. This is why our greatest tragedies are often laughable. Dignity always seems to find some way of disgracing itself.

—Aridity is the state we achieve not long after having done something notable.

—More often than not, a reader is a dilettante.

—Curse your kindest relatives for what gifts they have given you; vilify them, then you will never feel guilty for what they have done for you. The guilt experienced from vilification is less than the guilt for having received undeserved and unearned gifts. Of course, this only applies to individuals for whom scorn and repudiation are favorable to gratitude as a means of self-preservation and defense, since they either lack conscience, or their conscience is so developed such guilt might threaten their very existence.

—Every book is a little coffin; every library, a columbarium.

—What we often long for is a thing we have and do not know we have.

—When we are no longer anything other than what we've produced; what has become us in our absence, then by becoming known for a fixed ensemble of works, acts, and so on, we become limited by them. The anonymous are limitless. The known are fixed. They can become no more known than by their known sum. Eremites must understand this, if not consciously, then intuitively.

—By acquiring a history of culture, we create a culture of history. The culture of history is more curious than any other culture.

—Permanence is ideal purity.

—Voice is vulnerable to reduction by rhyme. Unless saved heroically by diction or idiom, voice may be otherwise obliterated.

—Idylls—the word itself is a lyric.

—I reread to once again experience the bliss of discovery.

—If we respond to another's need, it is our gift.

—In assessing Hart Crane, Malcolm Cowley claimed he never left his quest for a poetry of ecstasy to seek a poetry of wisdom. Beyond the comparatively minor, but nonetheless notable, inadequacy of an either-or fallacy, we might ask why would one direction be preferable to others? Must there be a choice? Are these not combined in the most admirable and affective ways in other poets? What Harold Bloom calls "impacted density" in Crane's poetry, attempting to rationalize obscurity, are those painful marks of desperation throughout "The Bridge" that materialize in a grotesque abuse of language condemning both poetry and poet into a chaos beyond rescue or redemption. What keeps Crane on the literary calendar is, alas, his reckless, tragic and thus romantic life narrative. What we seem to cherish is his engine, his heart. And this may be said of an entire category of poets. It is nearly a literary cult of hero-stock of which Crane is one of many. This is true of fictionists as well. Case in point: Thomas Wolfe, a metaphor for the American heart.

—By following desire without condition, desire will hand out far more suffering than anything it might have promised in the first place.

—So often it seems the most impressive and memorable literary works leave us with a strange sense of completion mixed with longing.

—Whenever I am in the wild, in nature, the first thing that comes to mind is its excess, which is only excess in my mind. Thus, it must be otherwise, but I cannot imagine that otherness.

—When individual talent, what is truly rare and unique, cannot grow within the cultural garden of its time, it must take root elsewhere, often in a place so distant it will live and thrive and die unknown to the garden of its birth.

—Judging by the volume of public statuary, no one celebrates themselves as do Parisians.

—Every poem has a subject even if the subject is its claim to not having one.

—Each time I return to a poem I love, I return to an eternal embrace.

—When one sets out to write for an audience, or to be known, then ambition becomes the tenth muse. It carries an axe and a bag of hearts.

—The poem is an abode.

—The future as idea—like the past—has no purpose other than to modify the present.

—Like material wealth, cultural intelligence is accumulative and transgenerational.

—When we traded romantic idealism for cynicism, we traded hope for despair. These should not be our only choices; there should be ample room for other engagements, other parties. Survival itself requires the species to regard itself as a romantic ideal; the collective hero in the face of certain disaster.

—The prose poem offers circulatory variations in recurring meanings and nuances that are more difficult, one might even say impossible, to achieve in formal verse. The reader may enter the subject in its fullest possible expression, as if entering a palatial room.

—The ultimate stage in the spiritual ontogeny of the individual is the acceptance of the unacceptable: the dissolution of personal identity.

—The artist of the most original creations may return at any point and for any duration to associate with populism and portraiture, local color, parody and caricature.

—No family ever had a sage. Corollary: when Gene V. Glass, originator of meta-analysis, advocate of literary psychology in education and psychotherapy, received an invitation from Lincoln

Northeast High School in Nebraska where he had been a student decades ago, asking him to assist them in finding a solution to some issues they were unable to solve themselves, apparently turning to him since his national reputation as a thinker and educational innovator would prove useful, he politely declined. He knew "what happens to saviors." It is highly unlikely, despite his significant experience and intellectual resources, that he could offer any solution that would be acceptable, or if found acceptable would be successful, regardless of its merits.

—In artistic endeavors—painting and music aside—versatility may be the least understood, and in literature, the last to be accepted, and when accepted, the least appreciated. An experimental novelist for example, should not expect to find success as a novelist of transgenerational family sagas, or if able, a formalist poet, nor should a populist playwright seek to become an acknowledged phantasy fictionist as amusing or as unlikely as this may seem. The ironist is not our local colorist; the combat journalist does not usually write light verse for children.

Numerous nineteenth-century figures come to mind; Thomas Hood, Leigh Hunt and Edgar Allan Poe are a few examples; reduced substantially for this literary sin.

Clifford Dyment notes that Hood, "in his lifetime, suffered for his versatility. He suffers still. For every dozen people who know him as a comic writer there are only two or three who know his serious work." Hood's status was cast with *Odes and Addresses to Great People*. In this humorous work, "The public liked him as a jester and was willing to pay him generously for being one," (Dyment). His best poems—"The Lay of the Labourer," "The Song of the Shirt," and "The Bridge of Sighs" deform his literary image; they do not fit with the role of humorist. The literary mind, that is its cultural consensus, regards such differentiation in genre as it might someone with a multiple personality disorder. Well, who's talking *this* time? And how is it that a voice that mocks one subject lauds another?

Leigh Hunt for all his notable work on *The Examiner*—the attack on the Prince Regent for which he was imprisoned—the introduction of Keats, Shelley, Robert Browning and Tennyson to the reading public, his translations, and as an editor of anthologies—would never be forgiven for popular and sometimes sentimental poems. *The Story of Rimini* that Byron praised, Hunt's anti-war poem, *Captain Sword and Captain Pen,* his contributions to reforming poetry in a direction different from neoclassicism, his autobiography, "[noted as] his best work and arguably the best autobiography of the century," (David R. Cheney,) his plays, and many notable poems of literary merit praised by the best poets of his day, (Shelley dedicated to him *The Cenci,*) cannot seem to be read without his light verse playing in the background, and cannot move him out of the "secondary writers of the Romantic period," (Cheney).

Should a formalist poet become seized by the notion of writing as a Dadaist, or a Conceptualist, or in modes less extreme, even though this would be highly unlikely, it would not broaden the poet's popularity; the poet—aptitudes aside—would not be accepted as a virtuoso, rather such attempts would work to lessen any achievements as a formalist. The reverse seems just as true.

Satire is unique in this ensemble, and I do not mean the satire of Swift or Voltaire. Its embrace by a writer casts suspicion over his other work. The reader begins to suspect the writer may have been putting him on, so to speak. This alone is cause for embarrassment and humiliation. It shouldn't be, of course. Unless poems are fashioned as a family, or as a thematic series, they should stand alone, even when gathered in a volume. An excellent case in point is Poe. In his career he created perhaps six notable satires; most fall in the hoax category. He may have paid dearly for this, and his reputation may be still paying for it. If we follow Poe's chronology

and read all of his work up until 1848 with the publication of
Eureka, and even after his claims (suspicious in themselves for their
grandness,) that it was his greatest work, and was "more important
than the discovery of gravity," the reader is left to wonder if Poe is
serious about this "prose poem" or if he intended to have the last
scoff. Scholars continue to argue the merits of *Eureka*; its capricious
insults of philosophers and scientists, the vacillating tone and
inflated scope of its treatment. Once such a work suggests—even
remotely—it could be a satire, a hoax, or both—can the reader
return to the author's other work unaffected? Has the reader not
been put on guard? Has the original openness and trust with which
other work was first encountered been compromised?

Literary culture has established a cognitive screen in this regard.
Writers are typecast. The recent fascination with polygraphies,
("Transitionary framings, a case")—conceptual book art, aleatory
text collage and the like, assume objects, their selection or
arrangement, or simply their presence, elicit sensibility, or act as a
reflector to the observer. This is not so much a case of including
genres, or cutting across them, but forming art that is without genre,
or beyond it. We might find in it elements of other art forms, and
claim it is a synthesis, but that would not be a fair description at all
simply because it would be grossly incomplete.

The book-length manuscript of poems similar in stance, length,
structure and so on, that includes satires will undoubtedly cause
discomfort in the contemporary screener, so much so that the
collection may be returned as a result.

Perhaps what is behind this is our quest to find a beneficent sage,
an ultimate guru, a transformer, an omniscient prophet. Such
figures are nearly always solemn. There is no reference to Christ
being silly, or amused, or to his laughter. The artist—and Christ—
should be given more latitude.

—Art cannot be sustained without the labor of others. This does not apply only to managing gallery exchanges, monitoring symphony schedules, editing manuscripts or compiling lists for pre-publication copies, but also to those masons responsible for La Scala, or the Bolshoi, the floor sweepers of the Louvre, the janitors of the Museum of Modern Art, not to mention those who create, develop and maintain electronic journals, sound and visual sites, the work of the most deserved, the librarians, virtual or other, and always, the translators.

—Should I long to miss the church of leaves, the nights' blue pages?

—In *The Sixth Extinction*, Elizabeth Kolbert writes, ". . . a hundred million years from now, all that we consider to be the great works of man—the sculptures and the libraries, the monuments and the museums, the cities and the factories—will be compressed into a layer of sediment not much thicker than a cigarette paper."

What lives with such an image? And from what mind do such images occur? Should we think that mind, our mind, is the only mind that contains eternal forms? The power to devastate comes from the reader who, in most cases, cannot see other life forms around him, or in the galaxy, or in the cosmos, that exceed in rate and mass our own lives and experiences, who cannot accept dimensional transformations. Such images encourage the romantic idealism vital in our younger selves. I have often wondered if such idealism should be abandoned as we grow older. If the sordid details of aging should be allowed to influence our earlier, dominant sensibilities, or perhaps should such things as age discloses, act to revitalize our earlier convictions?

—Is there a lyric that would carry us off stage and accompany us through eternity?

—If our lives are directed from the beginning by eager parents with strong goals, we may become resentful and angry. If we are not directed at all, we are the same.

—If our dramas circle about ourselves and do not include the cosmic drama, then we are restricted to the expressions of a lesser life.

—We don't pursue people; we pursue images. Ultimately, if we marry we do not marry the person, rather an image, and that is true of the institution of marriage itself. The world has a way of dealing with ideal estates.

—If the artist's life is a sad life because of his art, then his art has made it sadder still.

—In poetry, form at best, is a skeleton.

—Youth may have ideals, but not ideas; age should never run out of either.

—The poet as firefly. ("Fireflies at Harsen's Island").

—"A book holds thoughts and feelings; it has a body, a spine and a name. I love the way they feel and look and smell." (Frances Styrk, the protagonist of *The Writers' Circle*)

—Piano keys clink in the rain.

—When the flower opens, it shows its face to the world. It is an intentional act in every biochemical sense. In doing so, it opens itself the disasters of the world, and for its time, until demise is imminent; it rests in the realm of oblivion. Flowers continue to reproduce themselves as if to feed the great universal maw of disaster. Both forces it seems are insatiable; flowers proliferate and the great maw consumes. Perhaps the rate and bulk of profusion outruns or over weighs the rate of consumption.

—Even the best gifts are not always welcome. The givers are often denounced or punished for having them in the first place.

—Imagination *is* experience.

—The way people dress tells us how they view themselves in their age, historical period, and class. It tells us how they wish others to regard them.

—The poem creates the poet.

—The poet always carries in flashes and turns the delirium of intense animation, pacific caesura, and the oppression of the void. These states seem to tumble about; they may appear in a brief span or for a period that has no measure.

—The longer a thing is known its significance diminishes.

—In our speck of time, consciousness blinds us as light blinds us, as sunlight blinds, as Klieg light blinds the actor, as city lights blind, as the light of civilizations blinds.

—By the time we have arrived in our middle years, life has passed with such celerity that we may wonder why we were ever given a name.

—More often than not, the most practical and beneficial solutions are bypassed or rejected.

—Those who are fulfilled do not need expression; those who are troubled require them.

—In our age it seems it is more important to be known than to know, even when the acquisition of knowledge gives special joy that cannot be found elsewhere.

—Desperation—marks of haste—are found among the most precise and accomplished.

—The symphony of lost thoughts.

—Echo Arcade: my explanation of that pressmark is this: once the body has become home to the book, once the book has become the body, all other residues and resonances comingle, and thus one has entered the body-arcade. It is very much like looking at Paul Klee's "Howling Dog," (1928,) that unique aural mix of welcoming colors, soft and vibrant. ("Keening the Shades").

—We have the inclination to ascend in one form or another. For some of us it is more than a passing wish; it is a life's dream, and for a few, a compulsion. To rise above others should be a regrettable desire, and to rise above ourselves should never require the reduction of anything—or anyone.

—Ecological connectedness and unknown dimensional connectedness . . . When I walk up the hill at the back of my house which is usually about a mile from beginning to end, I often hear the sounds of birds. I've learned to imitate one of the simpler calls of the thrasher—one I cannot duplicate phonetically on paper, only orally—and I've either become something of a convincing mime, or the bird is playing with me. He replies. I reply. And it goes on like this. Sometimes the bird (I suspect there have been several thrashers with similar personalities as I've been walking this route for many years,) will flit from tree to tree following me just to continue our mutual calling. I imagine if, one fine day on my walk, I should simply fall over never to rise again, there would be within a very short time a feast for many birds and animals. We see this often in the ravine out back; animals regularly feed on one another; the rabbits are never safe from coyotes, the coati pack will hunt the bobcat, and the road runner will eat anything. It's a supermarket. So too, I imagine the thrasher, my aural companion would as soon ingest my cells as those of insects. The substance of those cells would be transmitted as food and energy to those of the thrasher, of his muscles and wings, head and heart, and would fly until my companion would himself outrun his life and his cells would be transmitted to other hungry birds and animals and absorbed in the same way. Knowing this, sense approaches the edge of unknown dimensions.

—Disengagement: it is as necessary to turn away from the drive to engage events and things, only if to face 'nothing' as is the drive to engage.

—Just about everything we believe, and those beliefs that either accompany or determine action, or those we have about ourselves, are shaped by the cultural mythology into which we are born.

—About a month before leukemia took my father's life, he changed his name. He had used his middle name since he was a boy, but then oddly, chose to use his first name which was also the name of his father, and no one knew why. After some speculation, and lacking an explanation from him, there is this from "Landings," ". . . his choice [must be placed] with the unknowable, an option that should be included in every conjecture, and as an outcome, at least equal in probability to all others if only because its presence composes the larger part of our condition, and that has given me much comfort on the coldest of nights. The stoics—and a fair number like-minded thinkers since—tell us that one of two things occur at death: either we are consigned to oblivion, in which case there isn't any cause for anxiety because we won't miss anything, or there is some form of consentience. Either alternative is drawn from our experience and for this the better for their defense. But isn't it fair to include among these the unknowable? What we think we know is a fraction of a percent of what may actually be. Although any earthly comparison would reduce this prospect, it might be similar to explaining this world of air to the embryo still sealed in its womb of water—experience that exists but cannot be communicated, that would never make sense. The unimaginable world."

—Faith must be based on the certainty of infinite and concurrent realities.

—Act is idiom.

—The failure to understand one's time, that is one's cultural milieu, results in the victimization of the self.

—The most persuasive empirical argument for other worlds is this world; of other lives, this life.

—How we are attracted to charm. It's as if we were born with such an attraction.

—There is a gift above the gifts of wisdom or genius or beauty; it is the gift of passion, and with the bounty of passion itself, purpose.

—Ambition has a way of becoming its own subject.

—It's as if I've been floating through endless layers of changing surfaces . . .

—Any serious statement seriously risks becoming its own parody.

—The marvels and fascinations of turmoil and elegance.

—The artist is one through whom the world breathes.

—Others are composed by us; what we want or need them to be just as we are composed of the wants or needs of others.

—We are cocoons of assumptions.

—Can innocence rise above the unicellular?

—Sculpting the past in human memory is one of nature's fine arts.

—Every gift arrives with obligation.

—We come from absence and return to absence. What is in between is all detour. What awaits us is the unknown night from which we've come. One might hope for detours. ("Authorial Intentionality and the Blue Delphinium")

—What brings the writer to his desk is the possibility of the impossible.

—Percussion has greater popular appeal than discovery. Corollary: In the popular mind, percussion *is* discovery.

—Why isn't character regarded as wealth?

—The final and perhaps the most important achievement of the writer is to become the book he has pursued. If the writer is blessed, this will never happen.

—Every expression that fascinates is wrapped in a body of unlikely associations.

—Plenitude. Why, when the world itself teems increasingly with diverse life, when we see at every turn its effusiveness, should we be so driven to add anything at all? But then we too were added; we too were additions to a most prosperous production. And as if this were not enough, we become collagists, putting together what already exists to place something else that is unnecessary in the human parade.

—In one form or another, out of abandonment, ours is a search always for reunification.

—The best estimates of astrophysicists at the present day—early 21st century—when considering the most advanced ion propulsion systems in concept, indicate it would take about 10,000 years to reach the nearest exoplanet, (if we do not consider nanoprobs, again still in development.) This is longer than the recorded history of humankind. The result of the awareness of the physical universe—its immensity—is like the birth experience itself, a mutual echo, each of the other. The message is unmistakable: we have been separated by a great expanse from otherness; we find ourselves, and our own planet far from midtown; in the Orion Arm, and this separation may have given rise to substitution mythologies and metaphysics. Our host, the earth itself, is so small it may as well be a cell in the oscillating tissues of trillions of light years, and spans unknown. And yet, in our best moments, there is the conscious sense of visceral and essential connectedness.

—Yesterday's tragedy is tomorrow's melodrama, and next week's romance.

—Usually there is celebration over a first publication, when every first publication is a death notice.

—We are all shades passing shades.

—Not every artist requires the idea of an external audience; most do. It is nearly vital. The concept of audience remains a static ideal, while its reality is in flux, often to the chagrin if not disappointment of the artist. The artist should not be admired, nor should he congratulate himself, for having attracted an audience as audiences exist for the expression of every human attitude and condition. Transient cultural dispositions, chance, mutual interests, spontaneity, all work together to allow the artist to emerge as a temporary personification of the audience-desire. Should he acquire notice early, he will live to see his admirers rise and fall, become stagnate, perhaps return but never to what had been the first great connection; the artist-audience consonance.

Yet from the beginning the artist—every artist—has an audience, the audience of the self that is pleased or displeased, encourages a change in direction from this way to that, or to move on, or to begin a project then abandon it just as suddenly. This is the only audience, the only critic, and the only admirer, that the artist requires, that will—for better or for worse—never leave him.

—Personification is the prototypical trope.

—Those most certain of their missions are often the most desperate, and the most desperate are often the most dangerous.

—In the complete poem there is a second poem that calls out to the first.

—Isn't the lie an indication of virtue as it points to the desire for innocence?

—Those poets who have chosen as their subject the subject of perception itself have become self-referential in their pursuits.

Many are notable, and yet their poems cannot be separated one from the other; their profusions are readily accepted as insight and discovery, when their unrelated metaphors clank against each other, and their texts are empty of Calvino's precepts; the poems hanging together in endless folds like old drapes.

—In his Translator's Note to a selection of poems by Hermann Hesse, James Wright includes a notable comment by Stephan Koch: "'Like everything else in his work, Hesse's thought is irretrievably adolescent, so that in his chosen role of artist of ideas, he is invariably second-rate . . . . Hesse's ideas are derivative, school-boyish . . . '" and Wright agrees: "I think Mr. Koch caught the nature and value of Hesse's art," and concludes his preface with this excerpt from *Steppenwolf*: "'Ah, Harry, we have to stumble through so much dirt and humbug before we reach home. And we have no one to guide us. Our only guide is our homesickness.'" Wright adds, "That is what I think Hesse's poetry is about. He is homesick. But what is home? I do not know the answer, but I cherish Hesse because he at least knew how to ask the question."

From earliest cave dwellings to the *Odyssey* to descriptions of celestial cities, the grand theme has been the search for home, for an abode, for a lasting destination, perhaps one that does not necessitate such awareness(es) as those experienced in this existence. Hesse sought an imagined reunification; his was a voice for the core longing of the species.

—Primary sense always exceeds expression, and expression with what it may inspire or stimulate, is forever pursuing it, and is always in its service. Primary sense is the progenitor of every muse.

PROSE SELECTIONS

TREE GARDEN

The day has been a residue of the night before. It rained steadily then, a fine shower through the early morning leaving the faint suggestion of moisture, like a ghost of itself, in the air ever since. The sky is the color of dull aluminum, a rarity in this part of the country publicized by the chamber of commerce as "The Golden Corridor," otherwise known to the locals as the desert basin.

It is late in the afternoon and it is late in the year. I have returned home from work to find my wife and our son off on errands in town and this leaves me with Cynthia, the Springer who greets me on the brick patio then reverts to her vigil in the backyard. I quickly learn that her watch has been uneventful. Normally the sparrows and finch are swaying at the feeder hung from a lower limb of the pecan tree. About the time they arrive, she chases them off only to have them flutter back for a few seconds before she spots them and the old pursuit continues. Not so today. Gone also are the hummingbirds who commonly gather at the glass tube filled with red sugar water attached to the trellis. I take my usual position in a corner of the patio in a wrought iron chair with a high back stamped with the impressions of grape leaves.

The atmosphere is at its stillest. A thick growth of cat's claw and honeysuckle cover the side of the house. Their leaves, smaller and thinner than most ivies, host a variety of insects, quiver constantly from the stirrings of underlying things, the trillion themes. As if the themes themselves are dormant. The leafy habitat, still.

It is like entering a hidden chamber, entering its long moment of inertia when all natural forces are equal, or at rest. The air is temperate, between mildly calm and mildly cool with a texture of its own, come forth with another class of climate in which it, and I, coexist. Here I am between lives. I too have become immobilized. In this condition it is clear there are two distinct and conjoining areas before me: the trees occupying the yards behind my own, cut to their upper regions by the block wall at the back of the property put up by Mr. Lopez, a type common to many neighborhoods in the southwest, and the frame of trees and foliage nearest to me.

This foreground was planted by the first owner of the house, a young attorney who found solace from the demands of his profession in his afterhours by working the place with his hands. He soon moved on, leaving behind several unfinished projects: a guest room improperly wired, a sprinkler system in need of repair, and this hastily begun green ark of singular specimens: the grapefruit tree which ripens in late December, the size of its fruit determined by the amount of rain it receives during the monsoon season, a class of evergreen, the Goldwater Pine, known for its ability to conserve water for long periods, especially through the torrid summer, the pecan that produces several pounds of nuts every year, and the mature fig whose leaves are the size of book pages, and have begun to turn yellow now it is mid-November. Each season, Mrs. Lopez makes fig jam from seedy, purple fruit and remembers us with a complimentary jar. In the furthermost reach of this foreground, in a corner of the wall, is a royal palm which towers more than sixty feet in the air.

A family of desert woodpeckers has taken residence in the crown of its dried fronds and periodically their hollow sounds—*thonk-thonk, thonk-thonk*—are heard as they drill for small insects in the soft bark.

When the grass—a cushiony St. Augustine the attorney laid down by hand as strips of sod—turns pale in spots, I ask Mr. Lopez over to suggest nutrients. Little of this suburb's landscape is indigenous, unlike the surrounding desert, where he grew up, the sand and bleached rock, the pear and barrel cacti, the stunted mesquite and ironwood, although there has been an effort lately from ecologically-minded groups to return to the original arid environment and desert scenery in the name of balance and what is most natural. So I wonder what he must think. If he disapproves, he would never show it. He often appears amused by it all. Maybe he is accepting the inevitable. But I will never know. He shrugs his shoulders, looks at me, smiles.

I continue the former owner's habit of differentiation. Recently I planted a pair of cypress near the back gate, then added some dwarf salmon oleander along a section of the wall. Next spring I may plant a five-gallon olive, but they take years to grow into an adult. How could this be explained? To Mr. Lopez? To anyone? Each tree has its own ancestry. The citrus may have come from California, the evergreens transplanted from the Mogollon Rim country, a half day's drive north of us, a relative of the pecan may have graced the gardens of the Alhambra, the fig from ancient Egypt, the cypress from a family that may have pre-existed Ephesus, or from a hill above Rome. Exotica. They are now in the American mix. Transplants, like myself. They will survive or perish in what the culture and the weather will allow.

And the weather this afternoon allows Cynthia to surrender her post, join the general inactivity of the place, stretch out on the lawn and doze off. She remains about twenty feet from where I sit, at her regular station, or midway between myself and the wall. It's always the same. The grass is worn there; she returns to the identical spot as though she had a tape measure in her head and marked off the paces to this particular location. She was never taught to do this, and I can only assume her behavior was determined long ago by her ancestors trained to give warnings from a fixed guard point situated the same distance from ancient fires and former masters long since vanished.

So the Springer must also be included in this frame bordered by the posts of the patio, open to the air with the exception of the white beams of the pergola overhead covered with the kind of dark green wind screen used on tennis courts. Errant cat's claw has made its way from the side of the house over much of the structure, hooking easily into the wind screens.

The background, what is in the frame, shapes distance: the upper reaches of mulberry trees, more evergreens of a bushy Scotch variety, and, with the possible exception of the sequoia of the western seaboard, the largest living things to occupy space, the cottonwoods and the eucalyptus. Their long branches abundant with leaves extend outward as if to know by touch or unspoken presence the subtleties of the region's atmosphere. Patriarchs of silence, innocent of their authority, they are made more authoritative. Surely others must be humbled by them. The re-creation of the dead: billions of organisms, former lives resolved and reshaped into the stateliest of organic figures.

In another month when the desert winter arrives and removes the last leaves from the deciduous trees, another background will be revealed, one seen mostly through the mulberries, through their bare arms frozen upward in desperation as if from an unknown aggressor. These, in the far distance, are unrecognizable, and appear simply as gray smudges in air. Beyond them must be other groups, and still others.

Poets, saints, and seers have always sought the consolation of groves, and some tell of an overwhelming grief that occurs in the presence of certain woody areas to suggest something of a kinship more than we know. In the early summer when I have had the occasion to travel over the high passes of the Rocky Mountains, I have seen clusters of aspen or birch on the slopes of hills, or tucked away in some declivity in a provocative display of light and shadow, standing over patches of late snow in a rich, secluded meadow offering irresistible solace, and I was drawn to them as surely as my own ancestors must have been to their forbearers if only for the security they offered and their protection from the more threatening animals and the capriciousness of the elements. I've pulled off the soft shoulder and stood outside my car to marvel at these arrangements, the spirits of the place, these creations of the dead.

Background-foreground. Inward-outward. A pulse-beat. The central motion of the natural world, or what I can possibly know of it, what I gather from my backyard.

The sky is darkening and it's become chilly. The dog has moved up to my chair and stares at me. Time for the evening meal. Soon the landscape will become reanimated, and I will notice it first in the living things closest to me. It won't be long before muffled voices will come from inside the house, my wife and son returned. There will be the clatter of a bread pan or a plate, discourse I cannot clearly understand, separated by the Acacia door, or the wall.

A drop hits a leaf. Then another. Soon there is the irregular pattering of rain reawakening the foreground; tiny notes of recrudescence.   A pair of doves in the fig tree who have been sitting it out flap their wings against the wet leaves like the sound of applause—either for the odd interim, or for the reunion with the more familiar. It looks as though the coming night will be a repetition of the night before. The rain will pick up again moving me indoors, and all the yardly things will return to their former concerns as if this period of rest, or indecision, or simply absence, like a momentary unconsciousness never was.

Later from inside the house I will hear a cry from a white screech owl, her signal that she has begun her nightly rounds. She will swoop down from the top of a distant cottonwood, glide over our house and out into the desert in search of prey. By morning she will have returned to her lofty home.

AMERICAN MIGRATIONS
(Selected Passages)

. . . . . After walking the streets, I arrive at the park and select an iron bench near the statue of General Stairns. Like the other statues, it is dark green, a kind of verdigris, with whitish streaks. These are from more than a century of snow and rainwater and frost. This image of a revolutionary war hero erected by the D.A.R. suggests a form in transition. Left unattended it may become coated with chalky residue until it is unrecognizable. A calcareous ghost.

The entire park is covered with a canopy of leafy elms and maples with occasional spikes of sunlight like yellow lasers breaking through to penetrate the grass or strike the cement paths. The place is unoccupied; the boys who chased each other on their bicycles left as I entered the grounds and I haven't notice any activity coming from the homes surrounding this patch of memory in the middle of town with its oversized statues stained with transparent time and the octagonal dance-and-band pavilion aging from disuse, and once, renovated with funds from the local historical society, as it states on the plaque, specifically, the chapter for preservation.

. . . . The viewing will be held in a remodeled nineteenth-century Victorian funeral parlor off Main Street on a listless Sunday afternoon in late August, in Herkimer, New York, in the Mohawk Valley, in the Revolutionary War Corridor.

. . . . The director stands beside the casket and makes the announcement that we are about to begin, then steps aside. Five men enter the room in single file. The first, the leader, has a thin black folder. In this is the text of the service, and he is the reader. All the men are in dark suits, wear white gloves and, about the waist, each has a flat, square piece of white leather with what appears to be an envelope flap in front. The third man carries one of these folded over his forearm. So there are five Masons.

But why this number? Surely not all of them have roles to play in this event. I recall the delight of Browne and Coleridge discovering fives in patterns of structures of plants and animals, in all natural things that carry this design or its variants, even noting that spherical bodies move by fives, (the coin rolled forward on a plane will cover exactly five times its own area in one revolution.) Perhaps the number of men bear some reference to the arrangement of squared stones in Roman and Gothic architecture—two above, and two below, with a middle stone, the *plinthus*. These form a structural body, stronger than its parts. The immaterial connection. A sacred geometry. But this is only conjecture on my part.

The reader opens his folio, and as he speaks, he frequently looks in my direction. The message is brief: my cousin is at rest now after his labor, in the invisible arms of a compassionate god. A feathery sprig of acacia is set beside him for remembrance and rebirth. The lamb's skin apron with its white silk cord, commemorating his loyalty to the ideals of his brotherhood, is laid over the edge of the coffin so it is balanced equally within and without. The reader confirms the deceased as a man of worth. He is deemed so by his service to others. Therefore, he has brought merit to himself, his human family, and to his creator. So elevated, the reader concludes, closes the text, removes the glove from his right hand, and approaches me. He expresses his sorrow over the loss of my cousin—and his brother—then shakes my hand, which his followers do in turn.

After everyone has gone, I am alone. The director is about to close for the night. I place a coin behind my cousin's shoulder, something for the river man, for a safe journey this time, (are we ever without tolls?) and then give my cousin a farewell kiss. His cheek is damp and cold.

When I leave the funeral home, walking down the steps, I imagine my cousin's casket being sealed shut at that moment, the image of his body removed from the world forever.

The religious service takes place the following afternoon in the First Methodist Church. The funeral director's wife escorts me down the aisle to the front row, directly in front of the bier. No one else is in the pew. The other mourners, his friends, are seated behind me. There aren't many. (Should we live to be eighty-eight, like my cousin, our social circle may be expected to shrink considerably.) The casket has a metal skin. It is dark blue, almost like blue-lilac, the ancient Persian symbol of brotherly love.

The church is very much early American, nearly austere. Dark mahogany is used throughout; the balustrade of the choir loft, the pulpit and the service railings. An exception is the stained glass image of Christ the Shepherd with crook and lamb. The face is featureless, replaced by an oval of white, opaque glass, in contrast to the colorful robes and the greenery in the background. When *The Lord's Prayer* is played by the organist, the vocalist is silent. The prayer is music. Wordless, like the face without human content.

When the hearse has its last passenger, the little motorcade heads toward the cemetery in Frankfort. By the time I get out of the limousine, the casket has been placed over the grave site. A breeze flaps the edges of the awning which has been set up to protect the mourners from the sun, or an unexpected summer rain. After the last words are said, and the minister closes the book, I take a few minutes to wander the grounds.

We are on a hill; the village may be seen far below. There's an occasional glint from the sun striking a piece of glass, the distant church spire, homes that appear tiny, partially obscured by a mid-day haze. Anyone who stands here is like a giant above a miniature. Once, when I asked my cousin if we had any other relatives in the area, he seemed amused, then said, "Yes, we do. But they're all up on the hill."

Although the funeral director is waiting—I see him standing by the door of the limousine—I visit the grave of my grandfather, an infantryman in France during the First World War, who suffered out the rest of his life from respiratory disorders, the result of gas warfare. There are the graves of some great aunts nearby, but the cars are filled with the funeral party and it is time to leave.

The low hills that surround us, this cemetery, the villages, the park in town, are dense with deciduous trees. They are so dark, they seem to be bluish-black. It was the home of those who predated the European settlers, the Onadaga, the Iroquois, and the Mohawk.

Like those who followed, they had their own legends and customs, their stories of wondrous deeds. Recent evidence suggests there were human groups in this region preceding the period when the American Indian dominated the landscape. Southeast of here, anthropologists have excavated sites and have found definitive evidence of the existence of these small human bands, although they are uncertain as to whether they migrated, or simply perished. These also must have had a history shared among themselves, a source of survival unknown to us. Perhaps there will be future inhabitants of this piece of real estate who will create and charge and shape their own fables. If we were to return somehow to this valley, ages hence, they would be unrecognizable, as strange as the practices of the Mohawk to his earlier indigenous brother. Or it is possible that those who come after us will have nothing to do with this property—by-passed by the human parade.

It is clear we are in transition. More houses are vacant; people have gone somewhere else. Those who remain, the current tenants of the place, the people on the streets, cannot be the descendants of the pioneers of American myth. They are like sleepwalkers, moving through some enigmatic, liminal presence. Borderlanders. The energy and stamina, the vision necessary for a life greater than the last, are absent from daily affairs. These are not the new immigrants; as for them, the Bosnians, Russians, and Jamaicans, few as they are, will they embrace the same essentials of a foreign nation as eagerly as the generations who preceded them?

Meanwhile, there is the struggle with disappearing things. We could sustain the losses with future promise, but this too is absent, at least today. Who cares for the ghost-statues in the park? Will what they represent remain? And what of the red-stone-heart of a court house in the center of town with its splintering white window frames? The committee for historic preservation placed the funds in the budget for repair, but there was a short fall, (the streets had to be resurfaced because last winter was so hard on them). Maybe next year.

SANITARIUM ON THE WISSAHICKON
(An Excerpt)

. . . . There is a stretch on the Wissahickon "with some of the most magnificent forest trees of America, among them which stands conspicuous the *liriodendron tulipiferum*," Poe wrote. When I ask a local arborist about a shoreline which might host a dense population of the tulip poplar, I am told this tree is abundant throughout the Wissahickon Valley. Nonetheless, I suspect a profusion of them along the rock out-croppings south of Poe's entry point. The tulip poplar may exceed 120 feet in height and has been known to live 450 years. I begin to suspect these may be the same trees Poe admired and that I am now in their company as was he.

BATTLE OF PICHACO PEAK
(An Excerpt)

Things—we humans mostly—struggle for recognition. What is it that wants us to be known, even for the briefest moment? What lies behind the vanity, the vagaries of wind and rain bringing the wild flower seed to the roadside; the tourists to the slopes? Whatever seeks affection is vulnerable. There is such a petalled sea of vulnerability here.

And what of the cousins, up in the peaks, don't they desire the same? If we move away from the shoulder of the road with its winding colored bands that will dry within a few weeks, indistinguishable from the weeds, if we move away from the flowers, there must be other, unknown things, whole systems which occur and pass away out in the heavens, among distant galaxies never known by anything other than themselves, or perhaps, whatever has sought their existence. What desires our presence beyond ourselves without which there would not be the blue or the gray, or desire itself, or the globmallow and lupine, or the affections of tourists? Things that must be known for themselves and for other things, this battle of the roadside wild flowers.

HUNTING THE THUMB
(An Excerpt)

Down the Sanilac County road from the swale lot there was an apple orchard near an abandoned farm house. No one knew who had once lived there, or what led to their leaving. There were apples everywhere, half-rotted on the ground, some still hanging on the trees when they should have fallen, and there would always be a couple worth eating that you could put away in a pocket of your hunting coat for later.

The house was wood frame, a single story, with a sagging front porch and two black, blown-out windows for eyes, and if you opened the front door which wasn't hard because it was loose on its hinges and the lock had been broken long ago, you could see straight through the house and into daylight on the backside because part of the wall was gone.

The day I was born, my father was hunting the apple orchard on the farm of the brother of a man he worked with, and stepped into a flurry of birds that rose into the air at once and the lead pellets sprayed into the flock one round after another from his 12 gauge pump. Only after he emptied the chamber, did he realize he had downed six pheasants with five shots. At the same time, my mother was in labor in a Detroit hospital, and was never as proud of the shoot as was my father, and never failed to remind him of it.

When he was an old man and dying of leukemia, he told me that was his "lucky day". The fact my father associated death and the celebration of the birth of a son in that brassy orchard filled with the smoke of gunpowder near a slump of a ghost house in season that would never return, I somehow understood, but could never explain.

It was like a dream that brushes against you and cannot be known in the morning.

GLASS
(An Excerpt)

. . . . The air was heavy with the scent of oranges; gold oranges and yellow oranges, oranges with coppery skins, oranges the color of saffron hanging heavily from their boughs as if waiting to be separated by their own weight, or the merciful hand of a grower nowhere to be found, who had abandoned the place, moved on elsewhere. The trees themselves formed an ancient design, so arranged in rectangles with a tree planted at each corner point and one in the center, so that the lines appeared at angles moving into the distance from any direction . . . . There were oranges on the ground too full and ripe to be held any longer by their hosts, so many they had to stepped around. They lay there from last season, or the season before, dark and decomposing. A flock of blackbirds gathered about some of the fallen fruit, taking turns pecking at the pulp, tearing at it with their beaks. There were other birds too, birds high overhead, and could have been hawks—at such height it was hard to tell—gliding from level to level, riding the thermals, then sliding downward through shafts of sunlight that held the colors of the orchard and could have been columns of silent music, before they pulled out of their dive, righted themselves to once again coast with wings outspread waiting for the next draft, or the next, to take them upward so they could repeat the performance all over again.

After they walked a fair distance, he spread the blanket out under one of the larger, more mature trees. The odor of orange musk was about them. It filled their heads with the disequilibrious sense of the orchard; detected only in blotches of sunlight; tiny dust motes, the residue of burst orange cells, drifting almost motionless as if for

the purpose of adding fragrance only, a contribution to the
confluences of floating debris from other seasons, particles of things
that were always in the act of becoming, stalk and leaf, deciduous
vegetation, and the undetected; particles of orchard matter too fine
to be seen, bits of being, remnants of other creations which had
settled here to become mixed and reanimated again by wind or water
or the vibration of sound—by some movement—in the warmth that
brought out the redolence of nectar to the surface of the fruit,
attracting errant, dull-headed bees that stumbled onto the place
seeking blooms to pollinate and were much too early, bumping into
spongy pulp as if intoxicated, into deaf mass nudging against itself,
density mixed with airiness.

GENII LOCI

As places change, the image of ourselves changes with them. Like we humans, their alterations may be anything from a nuance to something beyond recognition.

As an old man, Seneca visited his boyhood apartments at Ostia Antica, a seaport town at the mouth of the Tiber on the eastern coast of Italy, once considered the harbor of Rome. He recalled that when the house was built in his youth, the stone was newly cut and flawless. Now, as he moved his hand over it, noticed how it was weathered with pits, and the discolorations of time.

By first-century standards, sixty was old, and Seneca compared the disfigurement of the stone to his own body. He knew that nature had weathered him, and if he did not notice the changes in his physiognomy as quickly or as thoroughly as he had noted those of his home, it was only due to an admitted vanity.

Things could have been worse. Had he lived another fourteen years, he would have seen a more dramatic transformation in the homes and people of Pompeii and Herculaneum, about 150 miles from his beloved Ostia, in the aftermath of the eruptions of Mt. Vesuvius. It is not difficult to imagine that Seneca would have dismissed his personal reflections as insignificant in comparison to the destruction to life and property of that cataclysm.

Although the air was infused with dust and ash, it was nothing like a later event; the volcanic winter that occurred about 535 in Indonesia when Krakatoa was active, sending up miles of debris, blocking the sun's rays for months, creating floods, famine, and disease. It is as if nature must either destroy, or alter, its creations, no matter how refined or elegant. It must 'change them out' so to speak, at any price. This process seems unending.

We now know that both Vesuvius and Krakatoa were the result, directly or indirectly, of plate tectonics. The idea that the earth's surface is a crust floating on a globe of molten magma that is slowly hardening is relatively recent. While still in middle school, I recall the model of the earth attributed to some Scots' geologists and shown (by a confident nun) in the form of a golf ball. It was an image that was more reassuring than the notion of drifting continents. This concept was first introduced by Alfred Wegener in 1912, based in part on the theory of a single land mass that existed some 300 million years ago, that he called Pangea. The outlines of the continents may be seen to fit together as if taken from jigsaw puzzle. Wegener's views suffered from a lack of evidence and were dismissed until the 1960's when the discovery of ocean ridges and trenches gave credence to his hypotheses, and since, have worked themselves into popular belief. The fact that the surface beneath our feet shifts and creates earthquakes is disturbing—ask anyone who lives near the San Andreas fault—and that the human species is not as 'grounded' as it once thought it was, must contribute to the irony of our age, a fact that would not go unnoticed or unappreciated by the nun who taught a kinder geography. (She was fond of saying that electric light dimmed our ability to see the firmament clearly, as it was viewed in the nineteenth century, when the naked eye could observe 100,000 more stars than at any time since the development of artificial light, when each night, the sky revealed the truth of a heavenly world above.)

The natural reversals—the dissolution of place through subtle weathering by wind and rain, or by volcanic activity and shifting plates; more spectacular and volatile— are not necessary to change an area from a desirable location to an undesirable one. There are zones quite capable of developing in unattractive ways on their own, as though this was their purpose; antagonists in the Book of Locations.

The Salton Sea is such a place. It's California's largest lake, an inland sea occupying 380 square miles, the size of ten Manhattan

Islands. Although it is situated along the Pacific Flyway, and hosts 400 species of birds, it does not appear to teem with the kind of activity we might normally associate with such sites. There is a strange atmosphere about the place.

To fully appreciate this, it must be visited in summer, on a warm day, (temperatures reach 115 with 60 – 80% humidity,) when everything is listless, and the dead trees along the shoreline hold nothing. The water is heavy with saline, and seems motionless. The color ranges from a faded green (in algae bloom which offers its own distinctive odor,) to milky, especially in some of the inlets.

Along with the Sahara, and some peculiar stone mounds in Arizona's Painted Desert, I've never been in a place that was so clear in sending out its message, something actually *absorbed into the skin*. It is a no man's land, an indeterminate state to anyone other than the most avid aquatic biologist or birder. Here there is an atmosphere that is neither life or death, but dulled, seemingly eternal. If you stay too long, you have the sense you may turn to salt stone. The air alone with its stagnant smell is convincing, and the visitor feels a paralysis growing over him the longer he remains. Apprehension moves from negative awareness to a gripping anxiety. I suppose the feeling is similar to the trepidation some Europeans had about mountain climbing, even as late as the 1600's, fearing the ominous presence of evil spirits that lived in fog and crevice.

In contrast to these negazones, there are places that emit a perpetual effusion of spirit and enthusiasm, encouraging human delight. We cannot visit a human group whether residing in village or city, who cannot point out with pride, some sacred place near them; a well with purifying water, a field where levitation was performed or some other miraculous feat, a roadside shrine, a site of rejuvenation where we may experience a clearer presence of mind, transformation, *élan vital*, where body and mind act together to inspire magnanimity. The Sacred Groves of Ghana, Lhasa, Tibet, Mecca, Mt. Athos, Machu Picchu, Sedona, Lourdes, the sites of Greek and Mayan temples, sacred mountains, the grounds of the ancient or modern wonders of the world, or places still to be known, waiting to be popularized as energy centers, fields of electromagnetic activity where unexplained optimism occurs, where we are capable of attaining an elevated state, where we may become transported from our mortal baggage among energy vortices, were once regarded by pilgrims as locations inhabited by spirits, *genii loci.*

> There must be other inhabitants of the places
> we attend, enough to animate us surely
> with some residue, why else would we spend
> our lives among ruins? Why would we seek
> out city museums on rainy days?
> What is the central attraction
> of country villas, the roofless homes
> of abandoned towns, empty doorways,
> those painted caves of Altamira
> with their remains of ancient fires?
>
> Why this fall did we drive for hours
> to see the colors? How many deep groves
> of evergreen, stands of Aspen and bright
> birch called to us like memory itself
> standing among them spellbound with leaves
> clicking like the dry tongues of prior knowledge?
> It must be so. Why would we have stepped
> between mounds of sacred information
> in remote cemeteries to trace
> headstones with charcoal as if to reclaim
>
> enough of those figures who at last
> would lead us to the place these places made.

We remember our places. We reach out to them, and they are as clear to us as the heart's longing. Like Seneca, we enshrine them in memory. We set them down in poem and song; we photograph, paint, and re-create them. They are made into national parks, historic sites, and occupy untold niches of prominence beyond any monument, in our imaginations, for they are our most endearing companions, trusted and true, as if we could have never lived without them. While they may have the names of cities and streets and their own architectural designs, our dwellings surpass geography.

Ultimately, our homes, our destinations, remain invisible to us. They are those places to which we return again and again to become what else we cannot know, but the knowledge of their embrace and affection remains in a memory that is beyond time or body or visual form.

AUTHORIAL INTENTIONALITY
AND THE BLUE DELPHINIUM

We who are poets know that the reason
for a poem is not disclosed until after
the poem exists.

—Thomas Merton

TO HISTORY—

You will not remember me.
And I will not remember you.
So while we are keeping company,
please note the blue delphinium
climbing past the window.

When this poem was selected as a finalist for the 2016 NAR's James Hearst Poetry Prize, I shared the good news with a dear friend who happens to be a poet and academic; a product of a literary education, whose response was simply, "Why delphinium?"

I replied that the sound of the flower-word suggested to me both delicacy (*del*) and fullness (*phinium*.) A blue delphinium (as distinct from various shades of plum, pink or white,) reminded me of the blueness of Whitman's lilac, associated with brotherly love. The truth is, I was attracted to the sound of the word, its shape, just as I was attracted to the flower itself, to its vulnerable silky petals.

Troubled with my hasty reply, a few days later I returned to the poem. My speaker addresses the human concept of history as one would a companion. By the second line, it's clear we're done with each other, and that would be enough, but there's this nagging Other, "the blue delphinium/ climbing past the window."

It never occurred to me that the nectary of the delphinium is shaped like a dolphin until I looked up its etymology, (Gk. delphis=dolphin,) or anything suggesting Delphic oratory, or Delphic allusion, or that Delphinium was once a city defeated by the Lacedaemonians, or that the flower is poisonous and at the same time, is said to symbolize an open heart. It's more than doubtful if any of these were lingering echoes from earlier reading brought to a conscious mind.

I have since learned the delphinium is the flower of the throat chakra (Vishudda) in Tantric tradition, the fifth chakra (five lines?) associated with communication (speech and hearing) and with proper meditation before sleep is said to lead to lucid dreaming. The color of this energy wheel—the throat chakra—is blue. All this was discovered after the poem's writing, and I was beginning to wonder how much of what was unknown to me was already in the minds of NAR's readers.

"To History—" might be seen as serving as something of a slight *Ars Poetica*: it is the engagement with the unknown journey of the poem-flower on its way past the all-too-brief window of human perception. That engagement is everything to the poet. It is the reason why we might take any interest in the world at all. The poet is taken from the determined biological path (birth, procreation, death, the quotidian realities,) on the Grand Detour. The life of a poet may be seen as one of detours. The exploration and the connection of them is a life's work.

Until recently, it was generally thought that for a poet to discuss the meaning of one's poems would limit meaning. The more interpretations, the better. Seeds in the wind. But in this case, meaning arrived as a result of having written the thing. I do not find the meanings of poems in their analyses, but for their existence; it is how I learn their reasons. I do not know the sources of the poem's substance any more than I know the source of its flower which is the poem's center.

I have written many poems that no longer speak to me, but for the few that return, for those that show their transformations, I continue the conversation, learning what was unknown to me before. It must be so for other poets; a bow drawn across the common human vessel.

MANIFESTO:

ON

THE NEXT APOCALPYSE

OURS is an age in which the transcultural mind is nearly consumed by the prospect of global warming, greenhouse gases, and the consequences of such warming on ocean levels and seacoast cities, the carbonization of our atmosphere and other devastating results of excessive pollution created by our species. It is our apocalypse. It has become the great myth of our age.

- To speak or to write in any genre with the intent to persuade others regarding the perils of global warming *without considering the devastating role of human population growth is vain, irresponsible, and works against any hypothesis for meaningful contributions to delay those cataclysms that occur as the result of global warming.* The exponential rates of population growth drive an ever-escalating demand for necessary goods and services, and without green alternatives, the irresponsible production, and consumption of coal, oil and gas, non-biodegradable refuse, along with increasing deforestation continue unchecked.

- To speak or to write in any genre with the intent to persuade others regarding the perils of global warming, *without considering the magnitude of past global extinctions including the early stages of the sixth great extinction, or the Holocene extinction, in which we are now living, and our species has been living in for the past 10,000*

*years is vain, irresponsible and strongly suggests that most of our
species has no idea of, and cannot imagine, the scale, or the dimensions
of a global extinction, no more than we can imagine the effects of
geomagnetic reversals. The Cretaceous Mass Extinction which
occurred about 63 million years before our earliest ancestors arrived,
flooded 40% of the continents, increased sea levels 300 meters higher
than current levels, and increased global temperatures 6-14˚C above
those recorded today.*

- The fact there are countries, international organizations, citizen
  groups and individuals working desperately to reverse such
  cataclysms brought on by excessive human population, and the
  forthcoming extinction, *incapable of correcting the first condition,
  or objectively acknowledging the second*, should stand as a clear
  illustration of human arrogance; its inescapable
  anthropocentrism, and a vanity that excludes the realities of
  contemporary scientific thinking and geologic awareness. We
  are increasingly reminded of this cause in our ecological
  literature, romantic in scope, melodramatic in populist appeal,
  which insists on a grossly exaggerated role of human beings to
  reverse what is ultimately and unavoidably a case of recurring
  geophysical phenomena, or to our species, its last great disaster.
  In defiance of all this, to tenaciously adhere to the idea that our
  species may somehow reverse what it believes is an imminent
  tragedy, is both noble virtue and sad folly.

THE CANADIAN SOLUTION

Since Americans are engaged in a contentious dispute over building a southern border wall to prevent hordes of evil-doers from invading our country, we need to reach out for more credible, practical, and yes, imaginative solutions.

Have we looked to the north? Have we considered that rather quiet, reserved, if not altogether bromidic neighbor, Canada?

Here is a land of untapped wealth and resources. If the border hordes who threaten our way of life could only avoid the United States entirely—bypass our great land mass altogether—and enter Canada directly, look at the riches they'd find there: herds of naive elk and moose, free-ranging squirrels and rodents, social programs more humane than our own, and plenty of ice suitable for human dwellings, and innovative sculptures. A panacea!

But how to get them there? Here is what we might consider to be a reasonable and ultimately satisfactory answer: The Canadian Solution.

Instead of wasting billions on a border wall, let's build a bridge instead.

It would be built by free labor, constructed of no-cost materials, and monitored at no additional expense, (or very little) to the already over-burdened American taxpayer. It would truly be a win-win, as we say.

First, prison labor could be wisely dispatched to every large landfill in the USA. Simultaneously, they would be sent to shipyards, air parks, railroad storage facilities—anywhere we have stored outmoded, unused, or unusable shipping containers, airplanes, ships, computers—stuff we can't sell—and using these materials, begin to assemble a convenient foot bridge from the southern border—over the shortest land route—to our northern border with Canada. The bridge itself would stand as a cultural *apogee* for our time. It would show the world just how creative America could be with its trash. After all, isn't it time we called out for an end to our shame, for our unrelenting assault on our landscapes with landfills; the oceans with our nonbiodegradable debris? This is our opportunity to shine. In fact, such a unique span as the one proposed might well usher in a new era in art-waste management: aerial trashformations. Let's not shun our junk any longer, but hold it up to the world in clever designs with thought-provoking maxims. We can be proud once again.

Second, this project could be completed in record time by releasing the incarcerated; not only would they provide the necessary labor, but also the creative architectural methods required, under minimal (volunteer) supervision of course, and could be given additional training in material adhesion compounds, welding and so on. They could be used as well for actually monitoring the hordes, given the necessary tools, say, courses in human crowd control, mass movements of families, and the use of corrective force if necessary, including assault weaponry. This would assure the masses—those homeless fleeing oppression—of safe passage.

Third, the proposed span would begin in San Diego, the northern most point of entry from Mexico, to a point—on the US/Canadian border line—just below Calgary. From there, the new Canadian immigrants could be processed and escorted by Canadian Mounties to their new homesteads—which they themselves could claim at five acres per family—in the Northwest Territories. The abrupt climatological change accompanied by wilderness surroundings—and the complete absence of any familiar cultural reference—might even serve as deterrents for those considering making the trek in the first place.

There you have it! A complete, comprehensive, and no cost—or minimal cost, (prisoners must be transported to landfills, trained in human relations, and so on) solution to the immigration problem

that threatens our way of life. Where else could such an elegant,
humane approach emerge but from raw, unobstructed Capitalism?
Bravo!! Oh, and Brava!!

PRAYING FOR A NUN

Dame Consolation stands beside my desk. Her arms are crossed under her white scapular and she has an understanding smile.

Although Boethius' Dame is a personification of philosophy and its solaces, she is also a feminine form with human features, one I had met many years before I ever read the *Consolation* which contains many of the old verities found in Plato's *Phaedo*, an early source of those precepts taken up centuries later by church fathers: service to others, sacrifice, suffering and purification of the soul, and pursuit of the Good; the bedrock of Christian eschatology.

They were also evident in the daily life of Sr. Martin de Porres, O.P., (formerly Corinne Recker, 1928-1979).

Sister Martin, who taught everything a second-grader needed to know, or at least everything in the second grade curriculum, had been standing behind me for several minutes with her arms folded under her scapular. Sister was young and tall and pleasant. I was gazing out of a large classroom window at the leafy street below, daydreaming of the Flats.

"Michael, *where* are you?" she asked.

I told her. I said, "Sister, I'm on the Flats."

"I see. And where might that be?"

It was too late; I had returned to my other world and Sister never received an answer.

Whenever I wasn't daydreaming, I knew when Sister Martin was near. I could smell her habit. That is, the narrow piece of white cloth worn from her neck to her ankles, required of the Dominican teaching order, was heavily starched.

One summer, many years later, when I was trying to navigate the poetry of St. John of the Cross, and bumped into Teresa of Ávila, I first learned of "the odour of sanctity," and how it is said to linger about holy individuals, and not having any other reference, I remembered Sister Martin.

In her classroom, reading was a reward. Once students completed their daily math workbook exercises, they could read anything they wished to read. Of course, a book had to pass 'inspection', and if the student did not have access to a favorite book, one was quickly found in the school library.

Not long after the daydreaming episode, my mother received a telephone call. It was Sister Martin with her unanswered question about the Flats.

"It's where Michael and his father go fishing," she explained.

We fished in the winter months; went out far on the ice with shanty and spud. On the way, we passed small perch and bass frozen in wavy glass. They came to the shallow water late in the season for warmth, or food, and stayed too long, stayed until their bodies were too sluggish to return to the deep. As I stepped across them carefully, stiff in their clear winter tombs, I wondered if in the spring they wouldn't wake, shake themselves, and swim out to join the other fish that were concerned about their whereabouts and had many questions to ask them.

While I was dreaming about the next fishing trip, I was still in class, and there was math to do. I completed in record time the most complex mathematical problems ever to confront the second-grade mind. The first to finish my workbook, I was at the head of my class.

Sister Martin was nearby. I could tell.

"Michael, I see you have finished the assignment. And so soon. Let's have a look, shall we?"

She gave a kind smile, though it was a little sad. Sister knew what I knew, and what the other students didn't know: that I had scribbled down the first numbers that came to mind.

We had done this before, and Sister was beginning to understand that the future of mathematics would go on without me, and so she did the next best thing.

She returned my book about sea adventures and pirates and how a boy with unruly hair might stow away on a ship bound for an unchartered island and buried treasure.

At the time, for me this was simply an act of kindness. I did not understand its importance then, although through the years it's become clearer to me. Sister Martin communicated a silent message: that she cared more for an individual's intrinsic worth—and in my case, his reading interests—than what the individual could produce. In a few moments—the time it took her to make her decision—she had taught me about understanding self-worth, unconditional acceptance, and trust. And after 32 years of teaching literature and writing, I know Sister's faith and compassion were not misplaced.

As for mathematics, her influence remains beyond calculation.

For me to pray *for* Sister Martin would be presumptuous of me on many counts. Besides, if suffering purifies form, (". . . whoever suffers in the body is done with sin." 1 Peter 4:1,) then for her and those of her faith, her earthly agonies as a middle-aged cancer victim for more than three years must be a mitigating, if not an exclusionary, condition.

I never saw Sister Martin after second grade. I have often thought that memory sculpts reality, and its reconstruction is its gift: often working at my writing desk, I will stop for some unexplained vagary as if waiting to be born; look out the window, see myself praying for Sister Martin, praying for her presence, for her dream of the ideal Good, for her Company.

---

*A special note of gratitude to Lisa Schell, Congregation Archivist of the Adrian Dominican Motherhouse without whose assistance this article could not have been written.

Michael Gessner has authored 11 books of poetry and prose. From the most recent, (*Selected Poems*, 2016,) The Poetry Foundation selected several for its digital archives, (2017). He has been a finalist in several competitions including "Discovery/The Nation," The Pablo Neruda Award, and *North American Review's* James Hearst Poetry Prize. His work appears in *The American Journal of Poetry, American Letters & Commentary, American Literary Review, The French Literary Review, Journal of the American Medical Association, Kenyon Review, North American Review, Oxford Review, Verse Daily, The Yale Journal of Humanities* and others. He is a voting member of the National Book Critics Circle. Other publications and information may be found at:
https://www.poetryfoundation.org/poets/michael-gessner
or https://www.michaelgessner.com/
Gessner is married to Jane Catherine Rassicotte, a watercolorist, and has one son, Christopher , who writes for screen.

Made in the USA
Monee, IL
07 July 2026